BASICS
GRAPHIC DESIGN
01

Gavin Ambrose
Nigel Aono-Billson

Approach and Language

ava
academia

An AVA Book

Published by AVA Publishing SA
Rue des Fontenailles 16
Case Postale
1000 Lausanne 6
Switzerland
Tel: +41 786 005 109
Email: enquiries@avabooks.com

Distributed by Thames & Hudson (ex-North America)
181a High Holborn
London WC1V 7QX
United Kingdom
Tel: +44 20 7845 5000
Fax: +44 20 7845 5055
Email: sales@thameshudson.co.uk
www.thamesandhudson.com

Distributed in the USA & Canada by:
Ingram Publisher Services Inc.
1 Ingram Blvd.
La Vergne TN 37086
USA
Tel: +1 866 400 5351
Fax: +1 800 838 1149
Email: customer.service@ingrampublisherservices.com

English Language Support Office
AVA Publishing (UK) Ltd.
Tel: +44 1903 204 455
Email: enquiries@avabooks.com

ISBN 978-2-940411-35-1

10 9 8 7 6 5 4 3 2 1

Production by AVA Book Production Pte. Ltd., Singapore
Tel: +65 6334 8173
Fax: +65 6259 9830
Email: production@avabooks.com.sg

All reasonable attempts have been made to trace, clear and credit the
copyright holders of the images reproduced in this book. However, if any
credits have been inadvertently omitted, the publisher will endeavour to
incorporate amendments in future editions.

BAFTA
Small

Programme cover for the 2010
BAFTA (British Academy Film Awards)
ceremony. Tavis Coburn produced
this illustration, with art direction
by StudioSmall. The cover depicts
a scene from the movie, *The Hurt
Locker*. This was just one design
from a series of different programme
covers produced for the event.

Contents

Graphic design is a complex and dynamic subject. Far-reaching in its influence and broad-ranging in the creative skills it encompasses, it is an exciting and challenging area in which to study. However, without a basic understanding of some of the ideas and processes that underpin graphic design, embarking on an education or career in this area can be a daunting prospect.

The intention of this book is to introduce some common approaches to graphic design as well as the language and vocabulary inherent to its practice and study. A sound knowledge of these areas will provide the student with the tools and techniques required in order to create, develop and analyse new ideas in response to a design brief.

Is there anywhere better than here? ➔
Adam Hayes

Pencil drawing for the allotment show, a group art show at University College London Hospitals NHS Foundation Trust, UK. This design demonstrates both an understanding and control of the written word and also a sense of craft. We need to consider both 'what' we say, and 'how' we say it.

Chapter 1 – Context
This chapter will look at some of the debates that have faced graphic designers throughout history and how they have influenced designers today.

Chapter 2 – Ideas
Here, we look at some of the techniques used to research, generate and validate ideas in response to a design problem or brief.

Chapter 3 – Workshops
The creative processes available to the designer are numerous. Here, we look at some of them and how they might influence the eventual design solution.

Chapter 4 – Vocabulary
Conveying messages and meaning are central to visual communication. Here, we look at some of the ways in which meaning can be conveyed through design.

Chapter 5 – Responses
Experimenting with type and images will lead to creative solutions, but these must be tested, presented and prototyped. Here, we look at some of the ways in which we might do this, and the effect they may have on the outcome.

Chapter 6 – Conventions
A final look at some of the conventions within which the designer must work to give structure and order to design solutions.

This book introduces many different aspects of the design process and the vocabulary used on an undergraduate design study programme, with distinct chapters for each topic.

Headings
Each chapter is broken down into discrete sub-sections, which can be found in the top left corner of each spread.

Clear navigation
A simple navigation bar allows readers to see where they have come from, where they are and where they are going to next.

Idea generation

← Research **Idea generation** Idea mapping →

The best results are achieved by using the right amount of effort in the right place at the right time. And this right amount is usually less than we think we need. In other words, the less unnecessary effort you put into learning, the more successful you'll be... the key to faster learning is to use appropriate effort. Greater effort can exacerbate faulty patterns of action. Doing the wrong thing with more intensity rarely improves the situation. Learning something new often requires us to unlearn something old.
Tony Buzan

Lateral thinking

Lateral thinking, also referred to as parallel thinking, is a method of idea processing that encourages a person to discover or learn something for themselves. A 'heuristic' approach (experimentation, evaluation or trial and error) can be used to reach an outcome which has rules that are only loosely definable.

Lateral thinking was devised as a method of creative thinking by Edward De Bono and first appeared in the title of his book, *New Think: The Use of Lateral Thinking*, published in 1967. De Bono's approach is based around the idea that vertical or logical, linear and critical thinking has limitations. In order to facilitate creativity, De Bono proposed that conventional patterns of brain behaviour would need to be disrupted – formulating new ideas should not be left to chance.

Lateral thinking is centred on the process of reasoning and solving problems through an indirect and creative approach.

The Seed ◉
Futro (Slavimir Stojanvic)
By adopting a lateral approach to the problem, and with the desire to express a strong commentary, Slavimir Stojanvic at Serbian design studio, Futro, created this powerful piece of political symbolism. The design piece – a poster to promote a conference on the uprising of fascism in the Balkan region – features the Nazi swastika reduced to represent a seed, which, if left, could grow into something more potent.

42–43

Quotations
Quotations support and expand on the subject matter, from both a historical and practical point of view.

Each chapter features work from both practitioners and students, ranging from explanatory diagrams to creative work. These provide a viewpoint on graphic design in context to its study and exploration.

The workshop

The workshop environment affords the opportunity to experiment and play. It is also the place where traditional approaches can be explored and tested for their suitability for future usage and as a means to respond to an assignment brief and project. Workshops generally centre around the introduction of new skills, such as print- and mark-making processes and book binding. These workshops, or introductory classes, usually provide an individual with a unique learning experience and inspiration. Not all workshops necessarily focus around purely traditional skills. Digital workshop sessions, for example, introduce software applications and advanced image manipulation techniques.

Print making

Earlier, we looked at how mark-making and sketching might be used to create and develop design ideas, resulting in a single print or a single piece of work.

Print making is a collection of techniques (linocut, woodcut, drypoint, engraving, etching, screen printing, woodblock and letterpress) that enables the creation of copies of a piece of work. These processes also help to further develop mark making, which when exercised and analysed, provide opportunities for the manipulation of ideas.

Woodblock

Wood has been used for printing repeat text, illustrations and patterns on to textiles and paper for almost 2000 years.

Unlike other modern printing technologies, woodblock printing, and its derivative, letterpress, produce results that have a unique beauty and quality.

Woodblock posters ●
Anthony Burrill
These self-initiated woodblock posters were printed using traditional techniques. The eclectic mix of typeforms makes for a series of deceptively simple posters. Printed on to coloured stock, these statements are given gravitas by their sheer scale and attention to detail.

76–77

Text
Each section is introduced by a brief paragraph in bold and the section is then further broken down into sub-sections.

Captions
Image captions explain and provide information about the images shown.

Examples of work
Actual examples from designers, creatives and students demonstrate a design response in context.

Shown here is a selection of studio/design equipment you'll need to have with you during your studies to enable you to complete your assignments. These tools will become essential aids to you when you make the transition from the educational to the working design environment.

Having a selection of quality tools to hand will make the creative and production processes easier, and the results you achieve will be both more accurate and more purposeful. Familiarity with a good range of design tools will enrich your creative work, and will allow you to articulate your ideas quickly and efficiently.

1
Loupe (linen tester)
For close examination of printed material and proofs.

2
Erasers
A selection of erasers will be needed, including a cleaning eraser, a vinyl eraser for fibre-tipped pens, a non-etching eraser for drawing ink on tracing paper and a putty rubber.

3
Pantone book
A pantone book will be needed for colour matching between screen and substrate.

4
Pencils
A selection of quality pencils from 6H (hard) to 3HB (soft). Also, a propelling pencil for fine-line work and sketching.

5
Tape
Different tapes will be needed for making mock-ups and dummies of work. Magic tape will come in useful as it doesn't show up on photocopies.

6
Roller
For pressing flat paper mock-ups and dummies.

7
Knives/blades
There is no substitute for a quality scalpel (sizes 3 & 4), with replaceable scalpel blades (size 10).

8
Drawing pens
A selection of different weight pens, for example .35pt, .5pt and 1pt.

9
Cloth marking and paper marking
A selection of chalk and markers for measuring out on to paper, card and fabrics.

10
Type scale and clear caps measure
For developing grids and layouts – without relying on a computer.

11
Drawing and paint mediums
Charcoal pencil, charcoal, conté crayons, pastels, graphite, gouache, watercolour and acrylic can all be used.

12
Crops
For experimenting with the cropping and editing of images.

13
Glue
Different glues for various media, including a spray glue for paper.

Chapter 1 – Context

As both student and practising designer, it is important to develop and maintain an awareness of history and context in graphic design. Looking back across historical design eras, one can develop a reference bank of approaches and theoretical 'tools' for tackling design problems.

This section will look at some of the debates that have faced designers throughout history, as well as those that we face today. How do graphic designers see themselves within wider society? Is it a designer's responsibility to be socially aware? This chapter does not propose answers to such questions. What is important, though, is that as a student or a practitioner of design, you are aware of these issues.

It is often said that nothing in design is new anymore. Designers continue to plunder the design vaults of the past, searching for inspiration and validation of their design approaches. However, what they often end up with is a rehash or pastiche of something that was really only fit for its original time and purpose.

The Bauhaus movement and the modernist style that followed it spawned a design revolution considered by many to be at the very heart of contemporary graphic design.

What Walter Gropius and his colleagues started at the Bauhaus was not about style; it was about functionality and form and was really an ideology. Admittedly, some aspects of Bauhaus design are based on aesthetics, but they also contain a rationale and reasoning. As the philosopher Immanuel Kant wrote, 'thoughts without content are empty, intuitions without concepts are blind'.

Design for the sake of design is empty; it needs the backing of an idea with focus, and a sense of purpose for it to be truly successful. In our world of open-source technology – wikis, blogs and social networks – opportunities to create work with shallowness, based on laziness, assumption and presumption are numerous. The need for validation and reason is more important than ever before.

Styles, trends and fads will always come and go; they are driven by technology and the zeitgeist. But many do turn into established forms and approaches within the world of design, and therefore become marked periods within graphic design history.

As new technology and equipment has made designers more self-sufficient, the ability to transcend cultural and global boundaries has also increased. Designers can now draw influence from a limitless number of sources in order to respond to assignments and to produce creative work that will fulfil a client's needs and requirements.

Much work currently seen as 'contemporary practice' can be described as digital design. Over the years, this will become an observation of this time and of the era in which it sits.

Zeitgeist
the spirit of the time; general trend of thought or feeling characteristic of a particular period of time.

Postcard for an exhibition at the Bauhaus, 1923 ⬅
Wassily Kandinsky

The Bauhaus is best known as the most progressive art and design institution of the twentieth century. Its major aim was to encourage craftsmen and artists to collaborate, therefore evolving a new level of inter-relationships between art, design, craft and industry.

Context and history have a bearing on all design work. The origins of graphic design are deeply rooted in art, craft and architectural practice. The first recognised evidence of visual communication comes in the form of the pictographs and symbols found in the Lascaux caves in southern France (15,000–10,000 BC). From the Arts and Crafts movement, Dadaism and the Bauhaus to postmodernism, we can draw influence to inform our own design practice. Research and inquiry can, in turn, create new approaches and outcomes. The following selection provides an introduction to some of the key movements that have both shaped and affected what we understand to be graphic design today.

Expressionism

Expressionism (1905–1925) originated in Germany. Inspired by symbolism, fauvism and cubism, it moved beyond the objectivity of its subjects to focus on the emotions and feelings of the artist.

Dada

Dada (1916–1922) was started in Zurich, Switzerland. An anti-art movement, its formation came as a direct criticism of and response to the atrocities of the First World War. Dada means literally 'hobby horse' and 'father', but the term was also chosen due to its childish phonetics. Much of the work of this period was nonsensical and used found objects.

Constructivism

The Russian constructivist movement focused on geometric principles and basic shapes such as squares, circles and triangles (a theme later revisited by the Bauhaus). Some of its roots stem from cubism, futurism and Russian suprematism. One of its main aims was to depict mechanisation and the growing power of the machine over the natural world.

L.H.O.O.Q.

L.H.O.O.Q. ⬆
Marcel Duchamp

Much of Marcel Duchamp's work was typical of Dadaism. L.H.O.O.Q. was a postcard-sized reproduction of the Mona Lisa, on which he drew a moustache and goatee beard. It was an attempt to mediate between high and low culture, through the defacing of a cherished national institution.

Triangle, square, circle ⬆
The use of geometric principles and basic shapes in Russian constructivism was a theme later revisited by the Bauhaus.

Modernism

Modernism was formed around Western society's new and developing industrialisation, and focused on the experimentation of form, process and technique. The new economic, social and political conditions that emerged from modernism affected the worlds of art, architecture, literature, religious faith, social organisation and even daily life. It literally took people out of the fields and placed them in factories, in turn forging a new industrialised society.

Following the Second World War, modernism became associated with the émigrés who fled Germany for America and other European countries. Mies van der Rohe, for example, was a key figure at the Bauhaus until pressure from the Nazi regime forced him to leave Germany to live and work in the USA.

Modernist design principles had a major effect on typography, and on its application and usage, in terms of grids and layout, leading, alignment, spacing and proportion.

Jan Tschichold, a German typographer, book designer, teacher and writer, embodied the modernist design principles he saw during his visit to the first Weimar Bauhaus exhibition in 1923. He became a leading advocate of the modernist ethic and with his book *Die neue typographie*, created a manifesto for modern design.

Initially condemning the use of all serif fonts, he eventually rejected this doctrine as being too extreme and reverted back to the use of classical Roman typefaces. In chapter 4, we will further explore the basis and historical background of typography – along with shape, balance and hierarchy – all of which form the basics for good design.

German Pavilion at the International Exposition in Barcelona, Spain ⬆
Mies van der Rohe

A reconstruction of the building in which Mies van der Rohe first used the grid as an ordering factor. It was designed to be a perfect example of modernism in architecture.

The Bauhaus

The Bauhaus school was founded by Walter Gropius in Weimar, Germany, in 1919. Bauhaus translates as: 'house for building'. It was a progressive art school, combining architectural practice and design with craftsmanship. The school became one of the best-known and most progressive institutions for art and design instruction in the twentieth century.

Theories and teachings focused on the creation of new forms of design and construction that could be used for everyday living. The purity of the Bauhaus form in architecture led to flat roofs, smooth façades, cubic shapes and open-floor plans, populated with functional furniture.

The Bauhaus school's design sensibilities had a massive effect on the performing and applied arts, as well as on typography and graphic design.

After several changes of leader, it was closed by the Nazis in 1943, and many of its artists and teachers fled to the USA to continue their practice and teachings.

The Bauhaus continues to have a major influence on graphic design, with its pure geometrical forms and emphasis on aesthetic fundamentals.

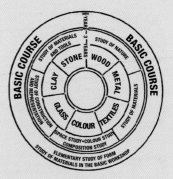

The Basic Course ⬆

The syllabus for the Basic Course at the Bauhaus was organised and developed by Johannes Itten. It introduced students to the basics of material characteristics, composition and colour. After successful completion of the Basic Course, students were introduced to crafts in the Bauhaus workshop.

'Universal' typeface ⬇

Herbert Bayer designed this typeface in 1925. Commissioned by Walter Gropius, it consisted of lower-case characters only. Bayer saw this as a means to express his views on modern typography and to create an 'idealist typeface'.

abcdefghhiklmnopqrstuvwxyz
1234567890

Akzidenz Grotesk Univers Helvetica

International typographic style (Swiss style)

The international typographic style, also known as the Swiss style, evolved and developed in the 1950s and introduced a form of typography that was concerned with cleanness, aesthetics and optical relationships. Core to its approach was the use of asymmetric layouts, strong grids and sans serif typefaces such as Akzidenz Grotesk, Univers and Helvetica. The typography in many early design pieces was the primary feature, with all other text performing a supporting role. As well as this strong use of type, the movement displayed a preference for photography over illustration or drawing.

In the mid-1940s, Emil Ruder, a teacher of typography at the Kunstgewerbeschule in Basel, Switzerland, and a pioneer of the international typographic style, based his teaching around the new functionalism he had seen at the Bauhaus. Ruder focused on the point, line and plane, and the way in which typography activated space. He believed in asymmetry, with an emphasis on counter, shape and negative space. Ruder said of his programme of studies in typography: 'We want good typography, developed from the intellectual, technical and economic prerequisites.' He also believed that typography should be unobtrusive and transparent, in order to clearly communicate the content of the text – a purist use, which excluded the use of any typeface other than sans serif.

Typefaces 🌐

Akzidenz Grotesk, developed and produced by H. Berthold AG type foundry in 1898, has a strength of form and clarity. It saw a revival in the 1950s with the arrival of the international typographic style (Swiss style).

Univers was released in 1956 by the small French foundry, Deberny & Peignot. There are still many differing opinions as to which is the true modernist typeface from this period; Univers or Helvetica (formally known as Neue Haas Grotesk). Helvetica was created by Max Miedinger and Edüard Hoffmann in 1957. Both typefaces were based on the 1896 typeface Akzidenz Grotesk and are part of the Haas Type Foundry's collection.

Dogma Outline
Dead History

Typefaces ⬆

Dogma, a typeface created by Zuzana Licko in 1994, was first seen in *Emigre* magazine. *Emigre* was art-directed by Dutch-born Rudy VanderLans, along with his Czechoslovakian-born wife Zuzana Licko. Their magazine was one of the first publications to be created on an Apple Mac computer and had a large influence on graphic design and typography throughout the 1980s.

Dead History was created by P. Scott Makela, a student and graduate of Katherine McCoy and the Cranbrook Academy of Art, in 1990. It is neither a serif nor sans serif typeface.

Sacred Heart sculpture ➡
Jeff Koons

Jeff Koons' Sacred Heart sculpture at the Metropolitan Museum, New York, displays many postmodern qualities. A sumptuous surface of shiny wrapping and ribbon alludes to childhood but is juxtaposed with potent imagery of the Catholic Church in the form of the Sacred Heart of Jesus.

Postmodernism

The term 'postmodernism' is so over-used now that it has become quite difficult to define its true origin and primary application. Postmodernism has been around for at least 50 years and is an inter-disciplinary movement. The movement sits in direct opposition to the purity of form found in modernism. It takes its influence from very divergent sources, mixing ideas with philosophy, different media and producing varied forms of output.

Postmodernism is focused around the search for a set of eternal or absolute values that can stand outside of any particular historical period or society. In the USA, after the Second World War, and later in the 1960s, Leslie Fiedler and Susan Sontag's writings and ideas inflamed anti-establishment views, central to the postmodernist idea. In France, philosophers such as Roland Barthes, Jacques Derrida and Jean Baudrillard, who were influenced by, but also critical of, existentialism, structuralism and Freudian psychoanalysis, began to construct a theory and language which avoided established modernist concepts such as causality and absolute truth.

Postmodernism caused design to grow up, and graphic design and visual communication drew immediate influence from the new technologies entering the design environment becoming enlivened with opportunity and importance.

A text is made of multiple writings, drawn from many cultures and entering into mutual relations of dialogue, parody, contestation, but there is one place where this multiplicity is focused and that place is the reader, not, as was hitherto said, the author. The reader is the space on which all the quotations that make up a writing are inscribed without any of them being lost; a text's unity lies not in its origin but in its destination.
Roland Barthes

The new wave

Spearheaded by the advent of the Apple Macintosh, the 1980s saw a wave in the deconstruction of type, structure and communication.

Katherine McCoy (co-chair of the Cranbrook Academy of Art graduate design programme), along with her husband Michael McCoy, developed new ideas and ways of thinking and doing, based on a combination of industry experience and Swiss typography/Bauhaus influences. She provided her students with a new set of ideas and the world of graphic design with a new discourse.

On the west coast of America, David Carson exploded on to the design scene. A world-class surfer, with a post-grunge attitude and little formal design training, Carson infamously set an interview with Bryan Ferry for *Raygun* magazine in Zapf Dingbats*. Carson, as art director, interpreted the piece as boring, concluding that a designer should not mistake legibility for communication.

Around the same time, also on the US west coast in Los Angeles, April Greiman started to integrate use of the Apple Mac into her design practice, harnessing its potential to pioneer new forms of digital visual communication. Greiman, a graduate of Allegemeine Kunstgewerbeschule in Basel, Switzerland, studied under Armin Hoffman and Wolfgang Weingart during the early 1970s, exploring the international style. Weingart's work was inconsistent with modernist heritage and much more representative of a changing, post-industrial society – he introduced his students to what is now referred to as the 'new wave'. This was a distinctly idiosyncratic form – an intuitive departure from the traditional Swiss form and use of the grid, which shocked many in the established design world.

In the United Kingdom, designers such as Neville Brody, Vaughan Oliver and Terry Jones began their own journeys to design individualism, based on possible postmodern experiences.

Globalism

Globalism or globalisation refers to the international trend of unifying organisations on a worldwide basis. Marshall McLuhan coined the phrase the 'global village' in reference to the analysis and future scoping of new media technologies in the 1960s. More recently, Adbusters and designers such as Jonathan Barnbrook have created work that contains social and political commentary. The content of their work demonstrates concern and conscience, and raises questions of social awareness and individual responsibilities.

A starting point for your research

This section has taken a brief look at some of the most influential design movements, and the effects they have had on visual communication and graphic design. These contexts and histories are an important part of any design understanding, providing knowledge and information that will lead on to further areas for study and inquiry. An understanding of them provides both a starting point and direction for the development of the design concept and idea creation stage.

Globalise this ⊕
Noel Douglas

This tour poster was part of an identity campaign for Globalise Resistance, an anti-capitalist and anti-war organisation aiming to shape and build a better world.

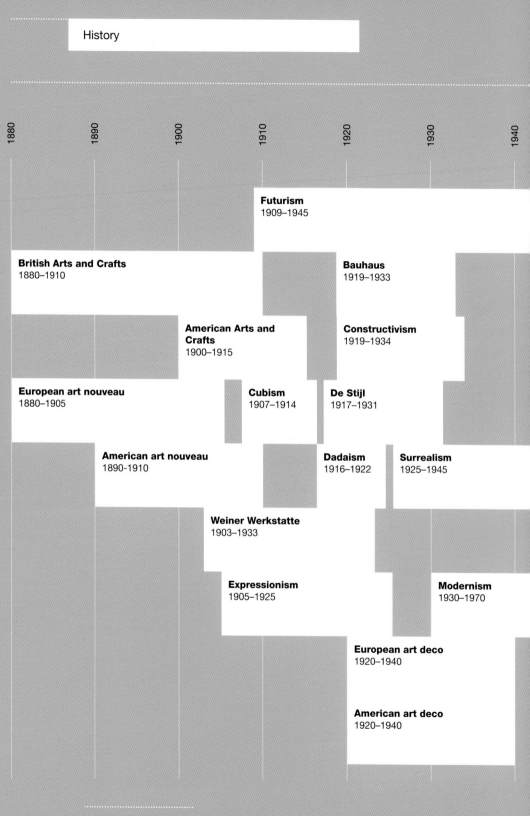

History

1880 1890 1900 1910 1920 1930 1940

Futurism
1909–1945

British Arts and Crafts
1880–1910

Bauhaus
1919–1933

American Arts and Crafts
1900–1915

Constructivism
1919–1934

European art nouveau
1880–1905

Cubism
1907–1914

De Stijl
1917–1931

American art nouveau
1890-1910

Dadaism
1916–1922

Surrealism
1925–1945

Weiner Werkstatte
1903–1933

Expressionism
1905–1925

Modernism
1930–1970

European art deco
1920–1940

American art deco
1920–1940

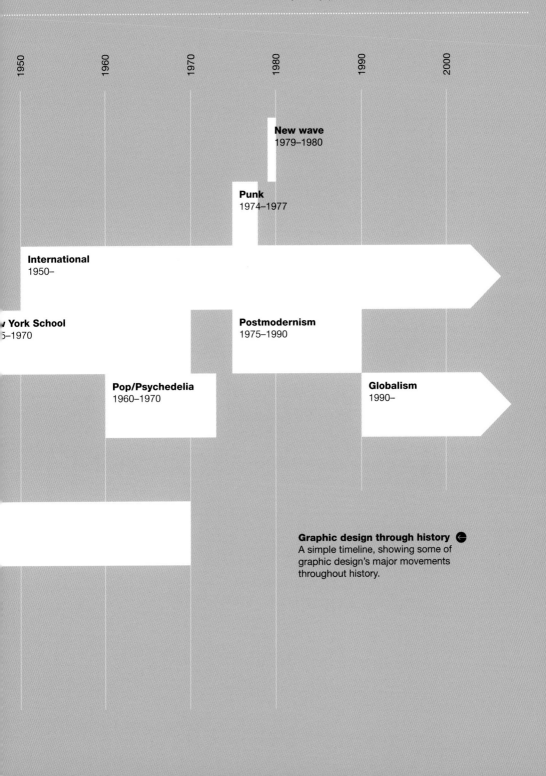

1950   1960   1970   1980   1990   2000

New wave
1979–1980

Punk
1974–1977

International
1950–

York School
5–1970

Postmodernism
1975–1990

Pop/Psychedelia
1960–1970

Globalism
1990–

Graphic design through history ◉
A simple timeline, showing some of
graphic design's major movements
throughout history.

In recent years, designers seem to have become more preoccupied with the need for a voice. As Michael Rock suggested in his 1996 article, *The Designer as Author:* 'Authorship may suggest new approaches to the issue of the design process in a profession traditionally associated more with the communication rather than the origination of messages.'

Does the role exist for graphic designers to be authors in their own right? It would seem that designers are increasingly looking to validate their position as individuals and creatives with a voice of their own, no longer satisfied with being anonymous and neutral in their position with commercially focused design activities. But with self-representation and authorship, there is always the issue of 'style' versus 'content', as designers try to create a platform for their authorship and standing amongst peers.

The designer as communicator

The increase in this form of self-representation seems to be driven by a desire for designers to be viewed in a 'higher' role. Ultimately, the designer's role is that of communicator – either as author, protagonist or simply as the provider of communication solutions. Whether the designer/author can be truly original is another issue. The design process does involve an element of compromise and client expectation, and for the designer to be a pure author they essentially need to generate the content.

Sculpture and typeface ⬆ ⬇
Eric Gill

Gill's sculpture at the front entrance of the BBC's Broadcasting House in London, UK, shows Prospero and Ariel from Shakespeare's play *The Tempest*. Eric Gill was a superb craftsman, typographer and illustrator. His typeface, 'Gill', commissioned for the London and North Eastern Railway (LNER), draws inspiration from his time working with Edward Johnston on a typeface for London Underground, and represents his attempt to make the ultimate and most legible sans serif typeface.

The evolution of ideas

Influences and inspiration for work can come from varied sources. The most important thing to do is to *look*, *read* and *watch* extensively. Keeping a notebook or sketchbook handy at all times is vital. Past and contemporary sources can lead to creative ideas and solutions. Movies, art, architecture and theory can all inspire, so a visit to a museum or bookshop may be well worth a trip. Magazines, television and the Internet give an insight into current styles and street fashions as well as into contemporary culture. Examining photography, illustration, film and social networks can give us insight and new viewpoints on the world around us.

By looking back at historical sources and art movements, unexpected outcomes may arise. Historical figures such as the Russian artist and designer, Alexander Rodchenko, for example, who produced a prolific amount of work that has influenced graphic designers since the Russian Revolution. Eric Gill, a British sculptor, typeface designer, stonecutter and printmaker, who was associated with the Arts and Crafts movement, has influenced typography and graphic design since the early 1900s. Countless influential individuals and inventions have changed our lives, cultures and the ways in which we communicate – when reviewed, these can influence the response of any designer and will often give rise to evocative communicative outcomes.

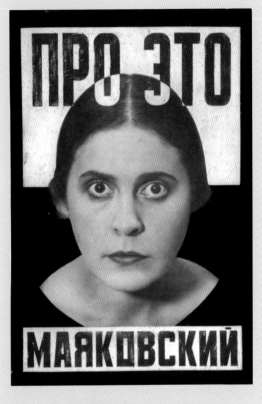

Cover design for the poem 'About This' ↑
Alexander Rodchenko

This cover was designed by Alexander Rodchenko, one of the key founders of and figures within Russian constructivism. He was probably the most versatile constructivist and productivist artist to emerge after the Russian Revolution. This lithograph captures the aesthetic style of the constructivist movement of the time.

...the man who is born into existence deals first with language; this is a given. He is even caught in it before his birth.
Jacques Lacan

Social attitudes, dissent and provocation fall easily within the realm of graphic design – from the 'agit prop' (propaganda) of the Russian Revolution to Ken Garland's manifesto of 1964, *First Things First*, which called for all graphic designers and creatives to consider and assess their position and role. Taking an ethical standpoint in relation to the commercial world, social effectiveness and sales do of course form part of design practice. But as graphic designers we also have a position of power, and of social responsibility. Graphic design has the power to persuade, to educate and to inform – not merely to sell washing powder or cat food!

First Things First 🔼
Ken Garland

The *First Things First* manifesto saw graphic designers express their social and moral concerns about the industry.

Revolution

'Agit prop' and images of dissent and provocation surround us on a daily basis – whether in the form of propaganda, from graffiti artists such as Banksy, or from established revolutionary imagery such as Alexander Korda's photograph of Che Guevara.

This seminal photograph successfully captured the anger and rage of Guevara as he spoke to crowds at the La Coubre protest rally. Giangiacomo Feltrinelli, a left-wing publisher and associate of Korda, used the image in murals and posters and turned the enigmatic image of 'Che the revolutionary' into a global icon, which has come to represent all forms of revolution and unrest. Today, it acts as a metaphor for counter-culture and holding an alternative viewpoint. This image has been heavily appropriated, appearing in many forms and graphic styles, as shown opposite.

Che Guevara, photographed by *Alexander Korda* 🔼

This iconic portrait of Che Guevara has come to symbolise revolution for many.

American Investment in Cuba ◀
Patrick Thomas

This sociopolitical piece creates a bold statement by subverting corporate logos to form a portrait of Che Guevara.

Graphic agitation and graphic activism

During the mid-1980s, advertising campaigns by the clothing company United Colors of Benetton used harrowing sociopolitical imagery to raise awareness of global issues. In such ways, graphic design and its allied communication channels, such as advertising, can play an important role in the promotion of national and international politics, global issues, liberation movements and charities.

Creatives across the world have become more conscious of the role that they can play as authors and message makers through their visual work.

Work and commentary in *Colors* magazine in Italy, in *Adbusters* in America or by Jonathan Barnbrook and Noel Douglas in the UK, explore and challenge people's perceptions, tackling subjects such as ethics, globalisation and industrialisation.

We all have to decide on our own personal ethical stance and the moral code that affects our approach to clients, commissioners and design projects. It is important to consider the wider issues that we will encounter throughout our career as creative practitioners.

Corporate Flag of America ⊛
Adbusters

Adbusters is a not-for-profit, anti-consumerist organisation, founded in 1989 by Kalle Lasn and Bill Schmalz. Known for its spoof advertising and subversive guerilla activities at the expense of corporate business, The Corporate Flag is a reminder of the power and influence that global brands have on society.

Colors **magazine** ➡

Benetton's research centre commissioned the influential American graphic designer Tibor Kalman to art direct *Colors* magazine. Launched in 1991, the magazine blurs the boundaries between art and commerce. Themed issues include beauty, race, sexuality or (as shown opposite) war and religion. Oliviero Toscani's approach to advertising imagery is as challenging and thought-provoking as the editorial content of the magazine.

Studio interview:

Lawrence Zeegen

Lawrence Zeegen has been an illustrator since graduating from the Royal College of Art in London in 1989. His clients have included international newspapers and magazines, book publishers, design companies and advertising agencies. During the 1990s, Zeegen was involved in establishing a number of illustration studios in London. He is now head of school at the School of Communication Design at Kingston University. His book, *The Fundamentals of Illustration*, was published by AVA Academia in 2005.

What made you decide to study graphic design/advertising/illustration?

I'd been in the top stream at school and even though I could draw (copy superheroes from comics), my teachers had encouraged (pushed) me into studying more academic subjects such as physics, chemistry and biology (all of which I failed or as good as). Punk rock came along in 1977 when I was just 13 years old, but it changed how I looked at life and I knew then I could be different – I just didn't know how. Failed attempts at catering school and drama school meant that art school was the logical next step, and walking into Camberwell School of Art in the early 1980s was a revelation. Many years later, I still haven't left – the British Art School experience grabbed me for good and I now find myself at the helm of a department of communication design. Why graphic design/illustration? From the Beatles' *Revolver* sleeve by Klaus Voorman in 1966 to the first issue of *The Face* magazine in May 1980, it was always music and style/fashion that gave me inspiration and drive. Studying graphic design and illustration was really just an opportunity to be part of a scene – designers had something to say and ways and means of saying it and I wanted a voice.

In your point of view, what are the key things to learn on a course or at college?

Some of the key things to learn aren't in an art school prospectus and where they are they're referred to as 'transferable skills', but they are really simply lessons in life and in no particular order:

growing up/bearing up

questioning/answering

looking/seeing

hearing/listening

learning the rules/bending the rules/breaking the rules

living and learning/learning and living

being creative/being uncreative

The few years at college are so jam-packed with new experiences, both good and bad, that learning to survive is crucial.

What makes a student successful at college or as a graduate?

Success is hard to measure – the certificate at the end of the course is not the be all and end all. Far too often, far too much emphasis is placed on the final hurdle and final result. Learning graphic design or illustration or advertising is not about acquiring a range of practical skills – it is about understanding how to communicate visually, having a voice, and having something to communicate: having a message and recognising who to communicate with; having an audience.

Being a creative practitioner is a way of life and not a job for life – successful students and graduates understand this and are self-motivated, self-sufficient and often selfish.

'The workload of the Attorney General' and 'Hope for Iraq?' ⬇
Two pieces of work created by Lawrence Zeegen for *The Guardian*.

Part of any graphic design course will involve an investigation into how images and texts communicate messages and meanings within the context of graphic design. Through this exercise, you will learn how organisations communicate to user groups/audiences and how this can be applied in relation to visual communication and graphic design practice.

Brief

Produce a poster or series of posters for the London Underground and Transport for London for one or more of the following situations:

- To promote an aspect of health and safety on London Underground.

  Escalator panel:
  W 419mm(16in) x H 572mm(22in)

- To promote travel on the London Underground to an upcoming event.

  Tube panel:
  W 609mm(24in) x H 279mm(11in)

- To advise passengers of the possible threat of a terrorist attack on London Underground.

  A3 poster:
  W 297mm(12in) x H 420mm(16in)

- To demonstrate how to purchase a ticket or how to use an Oyster card (travel card) using a series of sequential images.

  Tube panel:
  W 609mm(24in) x H 279mm(11in)

Note: Advertising Standards govern the usage of all aspects of London Underground's/Transport for London's corporate guidelines and their application.

These can be found on their website: <www.tfl.gov.uk>

Project objectives

- Initial sketches and magic marker thumbnails/visuals.

- Final poster designs.

Recommended reading related to this project

Heller, S. 2008. *Iron Fists: Branding the 20th-Century Totalitarian State*. Phaidon Press Inc

Hollis, R. 2001. *Concise History of Graphic Desig*n. Thames & Hudson

Itten, J. 1975. *Design and Form: Basic Course at the Bauhaus*. John Wiley & Sons

Lupton, E. and Abbott Miller J. 1993. *The ABCs of the Bauhaus: The Bauhaus and Design Theory*. Thames & Hudson

Meggs, P. and Purvis, A. 2006. *A History of Graphic Design*. John Wiley & Sons

Zeegen, L. 2005. *The Fundamentals of Illustration*. AVA Publishing

Chapter 2 – Ideas

The idea creation stage of the design process is paramount to the generation of visual communication solutions. By working through various methods of problem solving, a series of suitable design alternatives can be generated. These can then be tested for their suitability and used as proposals for a final design product.

To give validity to these proposals, it is important to have researched the context and environment in which they will exist.

Research supports and informs the correct approach to a design problem, enabling accurate visual communication. Design research, by definition, is the process or method by which we gather information about a subject. With this we can derive learning or appropriate information to formulate a response and define an outcome.

The inquiry or study is normally subject- or subject-area- specific. This research can, for example, be on a person, movement, technique, product or service. The research takes place through the means of reading, looking, testing, collating, editing, finding and evidencing all information discovered. These results or discoveries are usually collated into one central resource which, when reviewed, gives us findings that have a qualitative and quantitative result.

Qualitative research
Research that deals with the quality, type or components of a group. Qualitative research is exploratory in nature and uses procedures such as in-depth interviews and focus group interviews to gain insights and develop creative responses.

Quantitative research
Research that deals with the quantities of things and which involves the measurement of quantity or amount. Quantitative research allows actual numbers and physical dimensions to be applied to a group in order to accurately measure market situations.

The design research process will usually take the form of either primary or secondary research. The inquiry or research may take the form of case studies, trend research, performance and design improvisation, directed discussions, observation or experimentation.

Primary research ⬆
Primary research involves gathering information first-hand, through the use of focus groups and surveys.

Qualitative
Research that deals with the quality, type, or components of a group. Qualitative research is exploratory in nature and uses procedures such as in-depth interviews and focus group interviews to gain insights and develop creative responses.

Quantitative
Research that deals with the quantities of things and that involves the measurement of quantity or amount. Quantitative research allows actual numbers and physical dimensions to be applied to a group in order to accurately measure market situations.

Higher or further extended forms of design research become more formal and structured, often relating to the postgraduate or doctorate study processes, but not exclusively. They are a defined form of design practice, requiring guidance, and usually following a set procedure, resulting in a defined outcome that can then be published to an audience or to the world in general.

The point of research is to devise new knowledge and original thoughts, ideas and approaches that will contribute to knowledge and a further awareness of the subject.

Primary research

Primary research involves questioning an individual, group, community or organisation at the origin or source of information. Questioning can take the form of a questionnaire, interview or other technique that requires a direct response or reaction. The information or data is then collated and used to answer the research or inquiry problem. The object is to gather first-hand information, in order to fulfil the objective of the research exercise.

Secondary research

Secondary research, sometimes referred to as desk research, is the collection of information from books, journals and online or similar resource environments. Alternatively, the information may also be resourced directly or indirectly from companies, marketing, public relations, academic institutes, library/study centres or even databases.

Information obtained from secondary research is second-hand in nature but is no lesser in value than primary research.

How research relates to a project

Research can be used to define a basis for argument or as a back-up when substantiating an approach or idea. Having a sound body of research will enable the formation of a creative concept or idea that can then be developed further into a conclusive design outcome.

Secondary research ↑
Secondary research involves obtaining information from resources such as books and websites.

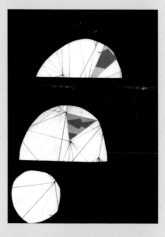

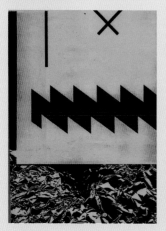

Once suitable research materials have been selected, the idea or concept creation and development stages can begin.

Creative thinking is a skill that can be learned and developed, and idea generation exercises introduce a variety of techniques to enable this: free association, mind mapping, lateral thinking, divergent thinking and sketching out ideas are just some of these.

It is important to consider the connections between visual and written communication in order to enable the generation of a whole range of innovative ideas. Incorporating found materials into the mix will further affect the strength of expression when producing ideas on paper.

There is no doubt that creativity is the most important human resource of all. Without creativity, there would be no progress, and we would be forever repeating the same patterns.
Edward De Bono

Several approaches, theories and schools of thought exist when it comes to idea generation. The following represent just a few and serve only as an introduction to the subject.

Free thought or free thinking

Free thought or free thinking is the process by which opinions are formed around a science, logic and/or reason. Free thought or free thinking does not accept or reject ideas unless they are directly supported by knowledge or reasoning. In effect, formative opinions come from fact, scientific inquiry and the principles of logic.

Possibility (hypothesis)

'Possibility' explains a concept that is not yet verified but that if true, would prove certain facts and phenomena. The term is often used in reference to mathematical theories, dealing with certain specific types of uncertainty (the opposite to probability).

Freeform experimentation ◖
Holly Wales

These process experimentations in form, shape and colour were created as a series of abstracted collage works using a mixture of media. The series draws on an understanding of freedom of form and construction, and has been developed on paper.

The best results are achieved by using the right amount of effort in the right place at the right time. And this right amount is usually less than we think we need. In other words, the less unnecessary effort you put into learning, the more successful you'll be... the key to faster learning is to use appropriate effort. Greater effort can exacerbate faulty patterns of action. Doing the wrong thing with more intensity rarely improves the situation. Learning something new often requires us to unlearn something old.

Tony Buzan

Lateral thinking

Lateral thinking, also referred to as parallel thinking, is a method of idea processing that encourages a person to discover or learn something for themselves. A 'heuristic' approach (experimentation, evaluation or trial and error) can be used to reach an outcome which has rules that are only loosely definable.

Lateral thinking was devised as a method of creative thinking by Edward De Bono and first appeared in the title of his book, *New Think: The Use of Lateral Thinking*, published in 1967. De Bono's approach is based around the idea that vertical or logical, linear and critical thinking has limitations. In order to facilitate creativity, De Bono proposed that conventional patterns of brain behaviour would need to be disrupted – formulating new ideas should not be left to chance.

Lateral thinking is centred on the process of reasoning and solving problems through an indirect and creative approach.

The Seed ➔
Futro (Slavimir Stojanvic)

By adopting a lateral approach to the problem, and with the desire to express a strong commentary, Slavimir Stojanvic at Serbian design studio, Futro, created this powerful piece of political symbolism. The design piece – a poster to promote a conference on the uprising of fascism in the Balkan region – features the Nazi swastika reduced to represent a seed, which, if left, could grow into something more potent.

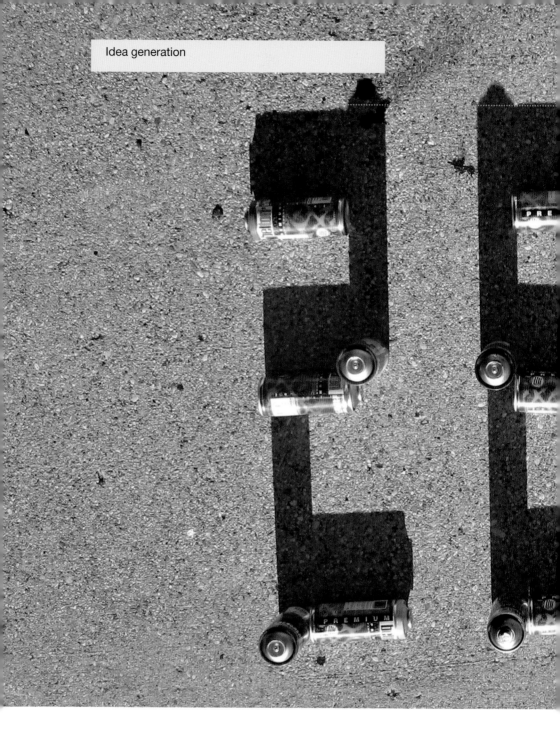

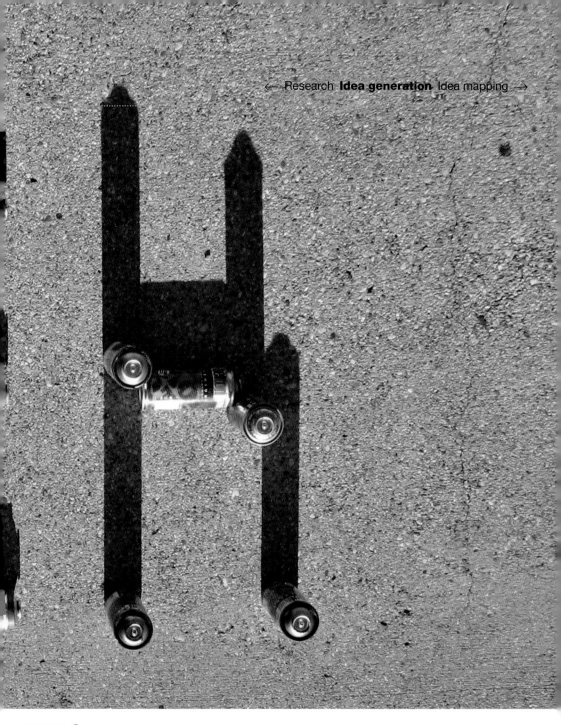

SPRAYZ ↑
Zek Crew

This image forms part of an ongoing body of identity work, which explores the use of paint cans as objects (rather than the paint inside) to form communication and meaning. A direct consequence of lateral thinking, this design makes type out of shadows formed by the objects usually used in the creation of the designers' street art.

Maps define and represent the whole or part of an area. Used to convey and depict geographic information, spatial concepts or scale through graphical representation, their content is an interpretation of the real world.

Idea maps, in the same way, are visual interpretations of ideas and concepts.

There is no such thing as information overload, only bad design. Maps are 100% content.
Edward De Bono

Early maps ⬆

A planispheric map dating back to 1858. At first glance, this map is a 'truth' – an accurate representation of the world – but in reality, maps have always been subject to political and economic pressures. Maps have been distorted and countries enlarged to represent dominance and imperialism over other nations. In this instance, is the map a representation of land or is it a representation of 'activity' and political ambition?

Geographical and spatial maps ◐ ◑
The original London Underground map (left), is linked to reality, plotting stations geographically; while the later version, designed by Harry Beck (below), is concerned with expressing connections and spatial relationships.

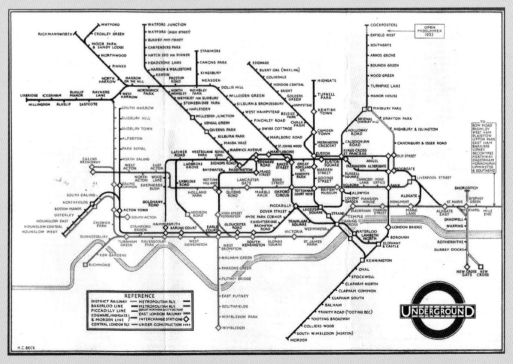

Mind mapping

Mind maps, sometimes referred to as idea spiders, are an immediate or quick visual method of understanding the structure of a subject and articulating ideas and research. They show how information pieces fit together and relate to each other. Mind maps can contain a large quantity of data but their visual nature makes it easy to analyse, remember and review. Mind mapping was popularised by Tony Buzan in the 1970s and has since been an important tool not only for idea creation and brainstorming but also for planning, problem solving and decision making.

The elements of each map are arranged in accordance with the hierarchy of their importance. Often, areas are represented by their individual or grouped meaning, along with their property or segment of information.

Mind mapping ⬇
Mind mapping is a useful method for producing answers through a visual process, sometimes including notes and visuals.

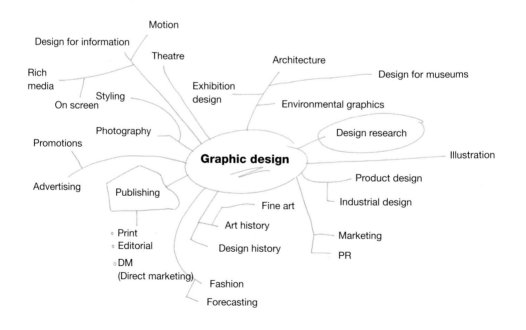

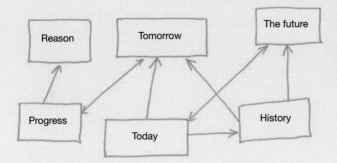

Cognitive mapping ◑
Cognitive mapping involves mapping the psychological transformations through which an individual explores, codes, stores, recalls and decodes information about their spatial or metaphysical environment.

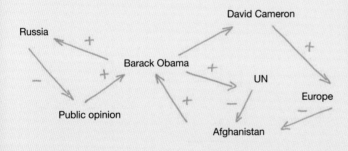

Influence mapping ◑
Influence mapping involves mapping the influences of individuals, circumstance and habitat on each other. It is often used to define goals and objectives, including negative influences.

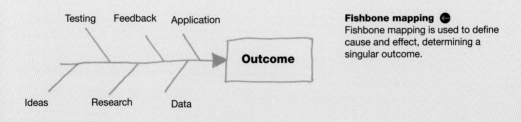

Fishbone mapping ◑
Fishbone mapping is used to define cause and effect, determining a singular outcome.

What can be mapped?

Most things can be mapped: places, businesses, galaxies, histories, bodies, philosophies, devices and even databases. The map is a culmination of calculated and verified data. Even a typeface can be seen as a map of the alphabet. Mapping techniques are not used exclusively during the initial idea creation stage – they can also form the basis of a finished visual outcome.

Adrian Frutiger's Univers font family, when laid out in full, becomes a map in itself, expressing the individual characteristics of each cut of the typeface. The numbering system, as shown below, acts as a legend to the map.

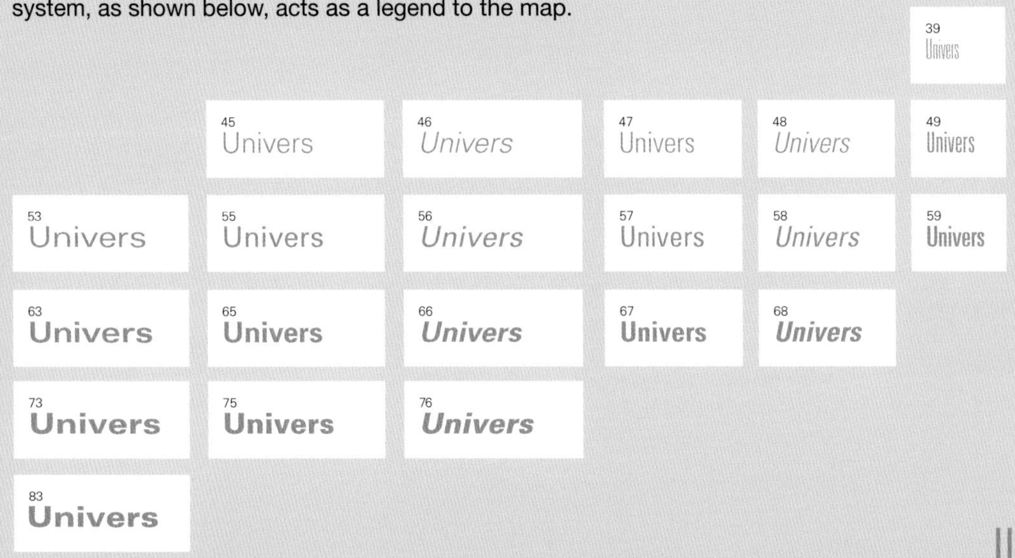

Frutiger's Grid ⬆ ➡
In this map, the numbering system acts as a key or legend. The first number describes stroke weight and the second number describes proportion. The second number also marks whether the type is roman or oblique: odd numbers represent roman faces, while even numbers represent their oblique counterparts. Further abstraction of this 'map' sees the letterforms creating a set of spatial relationships involving weight, proportion and angle (right).

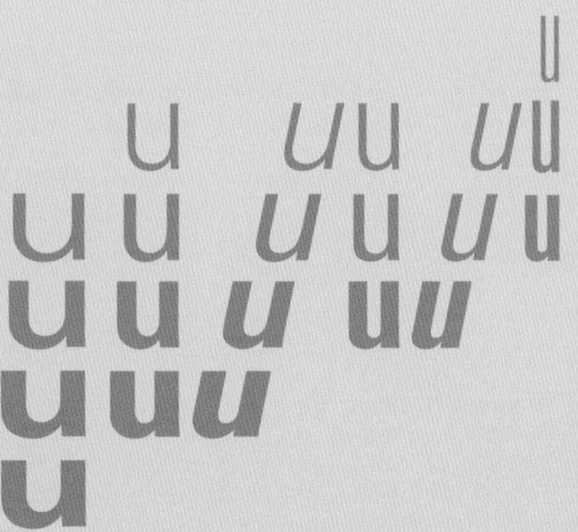

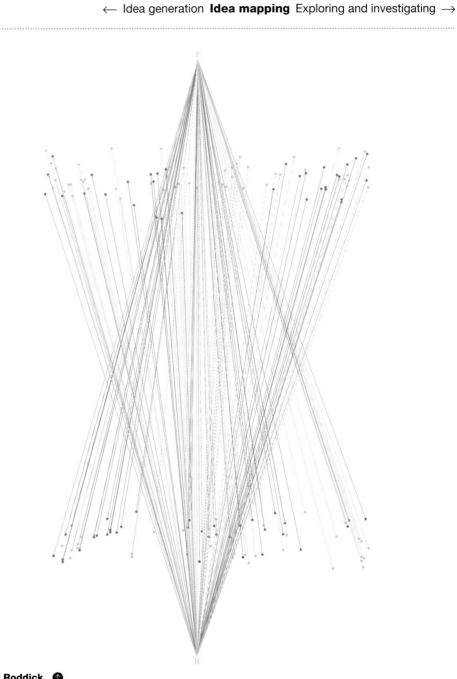

Federer v Roddick ⬆
Joel Wade **(a student at Canterbury College, UK)**

A visual interpretation of the 2009 Wimbledon men's singles tennis final
between Roger Federer and Andy Roddick, using a bird's-eye view of serve
statistics, results in a map or record of the game.

Blur - Song 2

Guitar   Bass   Voice   Drums

Transcription of Blur's Song 2 ⬆
Robert Kennett **(a student at Canterbury College, UK)**

A visual interpretation of the vocals, guitar, bass and drums performed during Song 2, by the British band, Blur.

Creative results need to be explored and investigated for their appropriateness and potential as solutions to the design problem.

By collating in-depth information and demographic, marketing or classification data, specific audiences or markets can be targeted. Research, testing and data gathering, in the first instance, may take the form of interviews with a client or company, the public, audience or end user. Design practitioners and other creatives can, in this way, uncover new information and new approaches to assist in finding a solution to the design problem.

A high degree of critical awareness and analysis is important in order for effective results to be achieved. All of this requires documentation and visualisation through written and visual processes. The need for an objective viewpoint is crucial.

Thorough exploration and inquiry can often lead to new and innovative creative results, as can be seen through the example shown here. The final piece is a clear manifestation of the processes described.

London Underground 🔽 ➡️
Anthony Burrill
Anthony Burrill's work for the London Underground exemplifies how to communicate a simple, hard-hitting message in a fresh and noticeable fashion. Safety communication isn't inherently the most interesting of subjects – commuters don't *really* want to read this type of information. The clever use of design and clear art direction makes for an accessible and engaging series of communications.

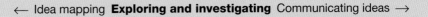

Gestalt theory

Good design is based on reasoning and contextualisation. As such, it is important for a designer to understand, explore and investigate the key theories that underpin the foundations of design. One such theory is 'gestalt'.

When describing the overall design piece, we often refer to it as the design's gestalt. 'Gestalt', translated, refers to 'a configuration, pattern or organised field that has specific properties which cannot be derived from the summation of its component parts'. It refers to a unified whole: in other words, 'the whole is more than the sum of its parts'.

In design terms, it is an attempt to describe the organisation of design elements into a holistic, unified and singular entity.

Gestalt theorists, however, are more intrigued by the way that our minds perceive wholes out of incomplete elements. The theory focuses on the perception that a singular entity is constituted of a series of parts, each with its own individuality. So, when these parts are brought together, they form a whole and singular entity. How does this work and what does it mean for design?

Gestalt aids the perception of a visual image, so that a clear message can be contained within the design work. Its principles are based on the premise of similarity, continuation, closure, proximity, figure ground and figure.

Gestalt
When the whole is more than the sum of total design parts.

These principles, where groups are formed, are there to add variety to the design form, which will create interesting results. The objective of their usage is to create a balance between either unity or variety. If there is too much unity within the design, it could result in a boring or repetitive piece of design work. Alternatively, if too many variants are used, the result may be chaotic and dysfunctional.

Having an understanding of gestalt principles will help you to control both unity and variety with a given design piece.

Before completing a design, the following should be asked:
1. Have all the key elements been identified?
2. Is everything connected?
3. Does it all work as a whole?

Similarity ⬆
This occurs when objects look similar to each other as a group or pattern. If a direct similarity is apparent, part of the group or pattern can be given emphasis, but this results in a deviation from the common rule, be it through type, arrangement or form.

Continuation ⬆
This occurs when the eye moves on or through one object to another.

Closure ⬆
An incomplete object or space, which is not contained. When there is a sufficient proportion of the space present, the viewer will fill in the missing bits to complete the whole and give it solidity.

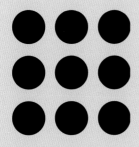

Proximity ⬆
This occurs when elements are placed close together. When two elements are placed in close proximity, they become one and work as a group.

Figure and ground ⬆
When the eye separates an object (figure) from its background (ground). This could be in terms of form, silhouette or shape.

Playing with this optical occurrence can result in interesting outcomes that either confuse or add clarity.

Figure ⬆
This comes through the playful intersection and interrelationship between elements. The viewer perceives the image as more than one thing at the same time.

In order to be able to share and discuss design ideas with others, they will need to be transferred from pure thought into some sort of physical manifestation.

Thumbnail sketches or drawings (small-scale renditions) are a quick way of thinking through the visual problem. Thumbnails can be very rough and are quick tests used for formulating an approach, idea, logo or layout at the start of a project. The production of thumbnails is an important part of the idea generation and brainstorming process.

By producing these quick sketches, it is possible to work through and evolve concepts, before making any commitment to any developed conclusions.

Designing with thumbnail sketches

Thumbnails describe elements and their location. They allow the designer to gain an overall picture or perspective of the project, from both a macro and micro viewpoint. Often more accurate than if created at an actual size, the design decisions and construction are easily shown using shape, balance and hierarchy.

Mark making can be very rough, as it is all approximate at this stage. But thumbnail sketches are most useful for giving an idea of proportions and placement. They can show optical balance of line, space and structure, the establishment of the concept and how the elements work together to form the finished result. Setting out all the ideas on paper in a linear manner means that a clear path of development can take place.

Generally, it is a good idea to produce several sketches. By doing this, a suitable solution will usually appear fairly quickly.

Concepts and initial design approaches should always be developed in this way, rather than attempting to work things out using software applications.

Macro
The large-scale or overall view of something. In terms of design, macro would refer to the entire design project, its scope, capabilities, application and usage.

Micro
The smaller-scale view of something. In terms of design, micro refers to the small details, individual scope, capabilities, application and usage of a design project.

Macro and micro scales

Thumbnails act at the macro level. They do not carry a lot of detail, but as a whole create an overall impression of the composition. They allow a designer to see the structural pace of the layout. Looking at the finer details at micro level will provide a completeness and fineness that is both harmonious and correct.

Macro and micro have an interplay within all composition. Composition itself is considered to be the sum of three parts: foreground, middle ground and background. Together, they form the three planes of vision.

The foreground

This is the visual plane that appears closest to the viewer. It represents all that is nearest to us or in front of the viewer.

The middle ground

This is the visual plane located between the foreground and background. It is the standpoint or area midway between both extremes of the foreground and the background.

The background

The background is the plane in a composition that is perceived to be furthest away from the viewer. Here, the scenery or ground is behind or beyond something. In a painting or artwork, it represents all that lies behind the objects in the foreground.

The scale of the objects or elements in a composition often correlates to their dominance. In design, it is easy to forget about the foreground and background, ignoring and forgetting about both the bigger picture and the detail.

By considering the micro or small scale, we objectify the idea; with the macro, we objectify the detail and the finish.

BVSS
IlovarStritar

Corporate identity and visual language for the
4th Biennial of Slovene Visual Communications.
This design for the Brumen Foundation functions
on both a micro and macro level. On a macro level,
the striking use of contrast gives an overall identity
to the scheme. On a micro level the imagery is
created with detail and care.

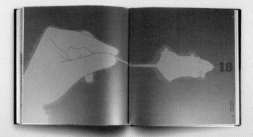

Working with graphic media is essential to the development of creative thinking and doing. Exploration and application of such media leads on to differing forms of image creation and/or illustration work. Mark making, drawing and image capture are all sensitive human activities that allow us to record the world we live in.

Basic mark-making techniques

Working with a basic variety of materials, such as pencil, charcoal, crayons, pastels, pen and ink, or brush with watercolour paint, gouache or acrylic, will allow for the examination of expressive techniques and processes. This will broaden and develop an understanding of visual communication. Meaning and emotion can be conveyed in either the most simplistic or sophisticated manner, depending on the approach and technique used.

An exploration of the various techniques, both traditional and non-traditional, and their outcomes, will allow new ideas to be developed, tested and communicated. Here, we will look at some of these techniques and their application.

Mark-making materials ⬇
Three commonly used design mediums: pencils range from 9H (H stands for hard) to 9B (with B standing for black). The hardest pencils are used primarily in technical drawing, and the softest, or blackest, are used more in sketching, giving tonal ranges and values. Also shown are blocks of watercolour paints (also available in tubes) and charcoal sticks. Each medium has its own subtle qualities, with differing results. Having a good range of mediums to play and explore with allows for a range and variety of expressive outcomes.

Hardest **Medium** **Softest**

9H 8H 7H 6H 5H 4H 3H 2H H F HB B 2B 3B 4B 5B 6B 7B 8B 9B

I PLEAD INSANITY BECAUSE I'M JUST CRAZY ABOUT THAT LITTLE GIRL

I Plead Insanity Because I'm Just Crazy About That Little Girl ↑
Ed Ruscha

During the mid-1970s Ed Ruscha created a series of pastel-on-paper drawings exploring a series of seemingly flippant statements. The typographical statements appear both innocent and slightly sinister at the same time. The typography is hand-drawn and contains subtle differences between each letterform.

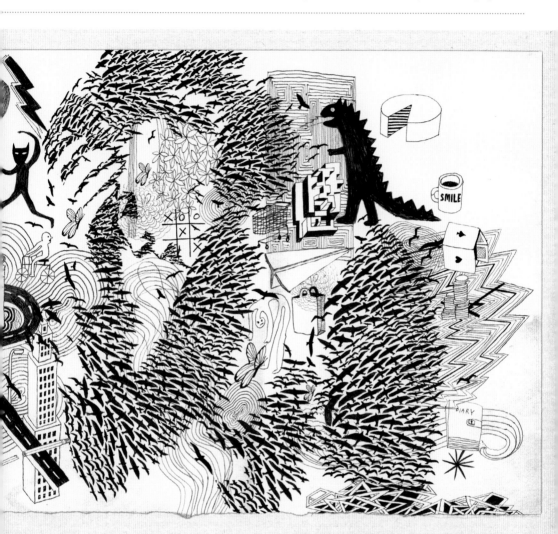

Samaritans Doodle Campaign poster ⬆
Billie Jean

UK charity Samaritans launched its 'Doodle Campaign' in 2006 to encourage young people to share problems sooner, before they develop into a crisis. The doodle concepts on their advertisements were selected by young people in focus groups based on the doodle's ability to most honestly and thoughtfully demonstrate their emotional state.

Sketching and mark making play a crucial role in the development of ideas and concepts. Generally, if the idea is right, you will know it. Your ideas in response to the assignment or client brief come from many places and through a variety of influences. The more you look, read and observe, the greater the experience you have to draw on. Compiling and recording these ideas and influences are important parts of the design process.

Investigation

By creating your own personal resources, you will develop an immediate source for inspiration. It is common for designers to create their own scrapbooks or reference reservoirs, containing collected ephemera: photographs, flyers, labels, tickets, business cards and other printed matter. These collections are great for helping with ideas, not only in terms of the imagery they might conjure up, but also through the inherent qualities that they might contain; the print processes, materials, colour or format that they might use.

Developing ideas

Creatives cannot force ideas, but through a process of investigation and by simply looking at other creative design work, inspiration will often be found. All ideas need to be explored and developed on paper through drawings, sketches and doodles.

Richard Brereton's book, *Sketchbooks: The Hidden Art of Designers, Illustrators and Creatives* contains an excellent selection of work, which should inspire any creative to put their ideas down on paper and see the seeds of their ideas evolve into a completed and singularly responsive series of outcomes.

Pen drawing of life study and sketchbook ← ↑
Charles Williams

These drawings observe and translate the figure and form, capturing its essence with the smallest amount of strokes.

Sketches are like embryos... As soon as they have been realised, they are born and start to live.

Richard Brereton

Early sketches

Concentric

Equal

Unequal

Overlapping

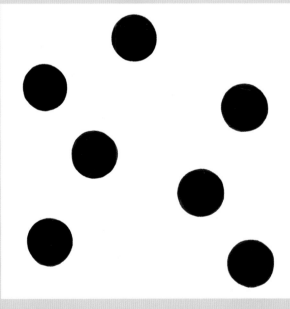

Final design

7 Circles ← ↑
Kavya Agrawal (a student at National Institute of Design Gujarat, India)

This project centred around the arrangement of seven circular elements in a square format, taking into account shape, balance and hierarchy, and an element of ambiguity.

The main explorations were divided into four major categories: concentric, equal, unequal and overlapping.

The final composition uses equal-sized circular elements to give balance without symmetry or monotony.

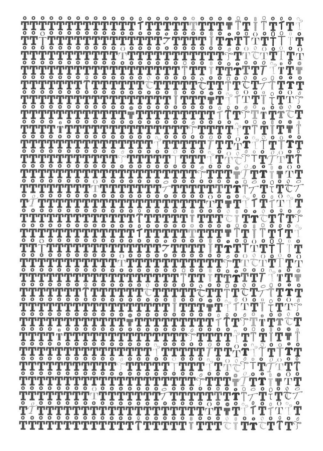

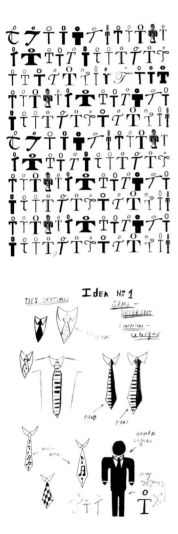

Common – Unique ◉ ⬆

Borislav Bogdanov **(a student at the University of Westminster, UK)**

Sketch work investigation and idea creation for a typographic 'antonym' project. The capital letters 'T' and 'O' represent the human form. In the final piece, the grey characters represent students of business, finance, law, mathematics and other 'traditional' subjects in the UK, while the coloured characters signify students studying creative subjects, such as art, design and media.

Studio interview:

Fred Deakin

Fred Deakin began his music and design career organising and DJing at club nights in Edinburgh. By producing flyers and visuals for these nights, he found his way into design. Moving to London to study communication design at Central Saint Martins College of Art and Design, he subsequently became a tutor on the course. In 1998, he launched design studio, Airside, with Alex Maclean and Nat Hunter. He is currently executive creative director there.

What made you decide to study graphic design/advertising/illustration?

I learnt my design skills through producing flyers for the club nights I was running. If the club was busy, it was down to a successful flyer. If not, I reckon it was because of a bad design. The flyers led on to me starting my own company, and then me joining together with a group of friends and forming Airside.

I don't think that having an art school training necessarily always makes you a good designer, but it does give you a context within which to judge your own skills.

In your point of view, what are the key things to learn on a course or at college?

Hands-on experience

Engaging with the outside world

An eye for composition

Interacting with an audience

A good set of technical skills

Having a clear vision

Students should be proactive and not reliant on parenting by tutors or staff; the best help from teaching staff is to get students to interact with the real world. A 'boot camp for designers' should be an important part of any design course, sort of like the 'Karate Kid' ethic: 'wax on, wax off'. Repetition, understanding and the gaining of some measurable practice.

What makes a student successful at college or as a graduate?

Putting your head above the parapet, for a start. It's tough outside, so you need passion, a skill set and a personality! Only you can 'make it happen', so you've got to create (some) of your own luck. People (designers/companies) will always welcome new talent in. But above all, you've got to really want it!

Malika at Airside, working on an alphabet of pin-up ladies, which later appeared in *Wallpaper* magazine.

Graphic pattern for a CD cover for the British band Lemon Jelly.

Maps inhabit the realm of fact, although not exclusively. They are figurative representations of dimensions, attributes and relations of things in the physical or logical world, reproduced at a scale smaller than life-size (usually, but not exclusively, their scale is 1:1 or, when mapping the microcosm, larger). For the purpose of this assignment, you need to consider the meaning of the word 'map' in its broadest terms.

Brief

Research the ways in which data is collated and expressed visually.

Part one

Collect data that will enable you to design a map or series of maps. Your chosen topic can be interpreted in the broadest sense. You might consider the following as a starting point:

- Sounds
- Words
- Devices
- Food
- Transportation
- Politics
- Images
- Networks
- Territories

Part two

Create at least one full-scale design piece. You should develop your ideas on layout paper to begin with. This will enable you to construct and formulate the way that your final piece might look.

You might explore a series of different approaches as a way of experimenting with your composition.

Note: you are **not** being asked to recreate a geographical map (in a literal sense).

Project objectives

- Development of research and data collection and collation methods.

- Development of methods for responding to data.

Recommended reading related to this project

Airside. 2009. *Airside*. Die Gestalten Verlag Gmbh & Co

Berger, J. 2008. *Ways of Seeing*. Penguin Classics

Brereton, R. 2009. *Sketchbooks: The Hidden Art of Designers, Illustrators & Creatives*. Laurence King

Harmon, K. 2003. *You are Here: Personal Geographies and Other Maps of the Imagination*. Princeton Architectural Press

Itten, J. 1970. *The Elements of Color: A Treatise on the Color System of Johannes Itten*. John Wiley & Sons

Tufte, E. R. 1990. *Envisioning Information*. Graphics Press

Chapter 3 – Workshops

This chapter explores the processes that a student may encounter through workshops. Mark making and printing are some of the different graphic media used to convey visual ideas. Processes encountered within the workshop environment are quite often essential to the development of both creative thinking and creative doing. Through experimentation, we are able to develop new ways in which we can convey our ideas.

Using different graphic media and printing processes, we see results with differing outcomes. With the development and understanding of each approach and technique, alternative forms of visual communication can be explored and experienced.

The workshop environment affords the opportunity to experiment and play. It is also the place where traditional approaches can be explored and tested for their suitability for future usage and as a means to respond to an assignment brief and project. Workshops generally centre around the introduction of new skills, such as print- and mark-making processes and book binding. These workshops, or introductory classes, usually provide an individual with a unique learning experience and inspiration. Not all workshops necessarily focus around purely traditional skills. Digital workshop sessions, for example, introduce software applications and advanced image manipulation techniques.

Print making

Earlier, we looked at how mark-making and sketching might be used to create and develop design ideas, resulting in a single print or a single piece of work.

Print making is a collection of techniques (linocut, woodcut, drypoint, engraving, etching, screen printing, woodblock and letterpress) that enables the creation of copies of a piece of work. These processes also help to further develop mark making, which when exercised and analysed, provide opportunities for the manipulation of ideas.

Woodblock

Wood has been used for printing repeat text, illustrations and patterns on to textiles and paper for almost 2000 years.

Unlike other modern printing technologies, woodblock printing, and its derivative, letterpress, produce results that have a unique beauty and quality.

Woodblock posters ➡
Anthony Burrill

These self-initiated woodblock posters were printed using traditional techniques. The eclectic mix of typeforms makes for a series of deceptively simple posters. Printed on to coloured stock, these statements are given gravitas by their sheer scale and attention to detail.

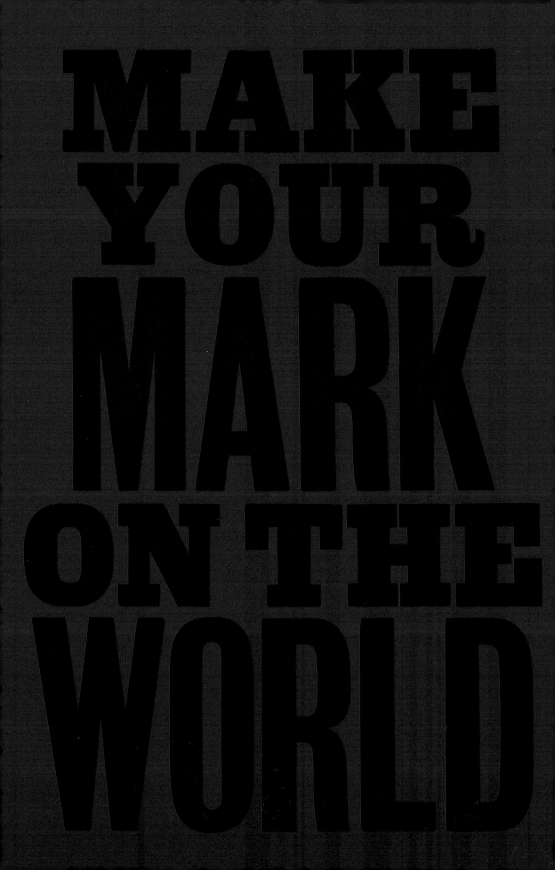

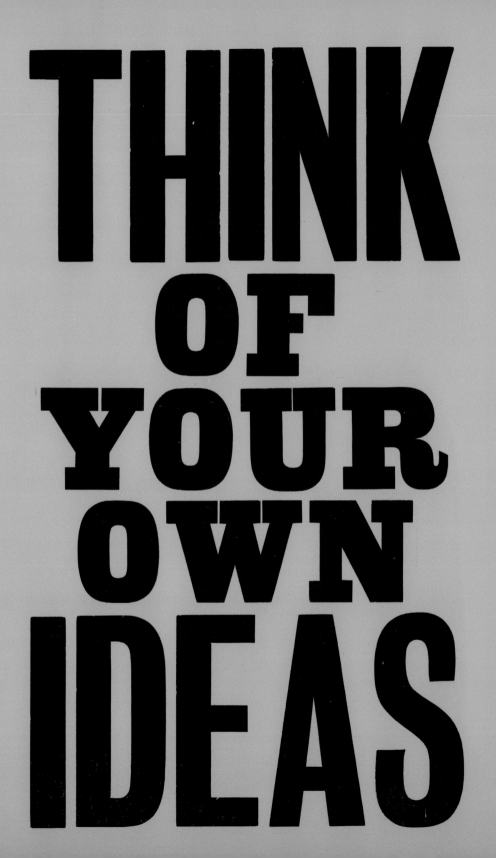

 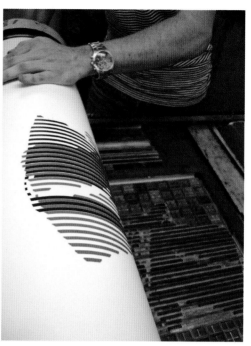

Letterpress

This is one of the oldest forms of printing (Johannes Gutenberg established the first book printing press in around 1450 in Germany) and works on a 'relief' type process. Letterpress printing uses type and images that are raised above the non-printing areas. Each print exerts variable amounts of pressure on to the substrate, depending on the size and image elements.

Letterpress was the first commercial form of printing to be used with movable type. The metal-cast characters were produced prior to printing and all image work was etched or engraved into a plate.

In order to master this technique, an understanding of the capabilities and advantages of the medium is essential. Knowledge of the inking process and how papers and inks will react, for example, is vital if effective results are to be achieved.

Jekyll and Hyde ⬅ ⬆
Alberto Hernández
(a student at London College of Communication)

This poster is made using letterpress printing methods and is based on lenticular images. Two perspectives are printed using interspersed stripes. The story of Dr Jekyll and Mr Hyde suited the brief perfectly.

Offset lithography or computer-to-plate (CTP)

Offset lithography uses a flexible aluminium printing plate coated with a photosensitive emulsion. When exposed to UV light, a photographic negative image is transferred on to the surface of the printing plate. The reverse-faced image appears on the emulsion following development, and this can then be used to print from. Alternatively, the image can be created directly on the emulsion surface of the printing plate, using laser imaging via a computer-to-plate (CPT) device called a platesetter.

The plate is fixed to a cylinder and water is applied via dampening rollers. The water is repelled by the areas of the plate covered in emulsion and so covers the blank portions of the plate only. Ink is then applied, via inking rollers, but it adheres only to the areas covered by emulsion.

The plate is then rolled against a cyclinder, which squeezes away the water, picks up the ink and transfers it on to the substrate through pressure.

This process is known as offset lithography and is mainly used to print books, newspapers, leaflets, posters and packaging.

Found, Shared: The magazine photowork catalogue ➡
Nigel Aono-Billson

Designed for David Brittain's 'meta-magazine', an exhibition that investigated the shift towards magazine art and the importance of the 'found' image, this catalogue was printed using full-colour offset lithography.

Digital

With the advent of computers, we have seen the development and increased use of ink-jet and laser-print processes. These processes differ from the traditional methods of 'ink on paper' in that they don't require a printing plate.

The ink or toner from a digital printer does not sink into the substrate as with conventional inking processes – it forms a thin layer on the surface only. In some cases, the ink or toner is fused to the substrate using a heat process (toner) or UV curing process (ink).

As it is cheap to set up and has low running costs, digital printing has become a rapidly expanding area, enabling the production of cheaper and faster print runs.

IN SOME
COUNTRIES
YOU
WOULDN'T
HAVE THE
RIGHT TO
VISIT THIS
EXHIBITION
ABOUT YOUR
RIGHTS

BRITISH LIBRARY

TAKING LIBERTIES
THE STRUGGLE FOR BRITAIN'S
FREEDOMS AND RIGHTS

31st October 2008 – 1st March 2009
⊖≋ King's Cross, St. Pancras and Euston
www.bl.uk/takingliberties

Silk-screen printing or serigraphy

Silk-screen printing traditionally involves using a silk printing mesh. However, synthetic materials now tend to be used in place of silk. The process involves the use of stencils to withhold ink and mask non-image areas. Screens are flat and can vary in size, but some are also cylindrical, as with rotor printing.

Ink or paint is drawn over the mesh using an implement called a squeegee and is forced through and on to the substrate or fabric below. There are several ways of producing the stencil: either by hand, cutting a design from a non-porous material and attaching it to the screen, or alternatively by painting the negative image on to the screen using a filler material that is impermeable. An alternative method would be the use of a light-sensitive emulsion which sets following exposure to a UV light source, allowing the ink to pass through the open areas of the screen.

Taking Liberties ⬅ ⬆
Anthony Burrill

A press and poster campaign for an exhibition at the British Library in London, questioning how we view our rights and freedoms. These simple silk-screen prints ask poignant questions of the viewer and present forceful and persuasive statements. Although this poster was ultimately printed en masse using lithography, the original artwork was silk-screened and then scanned for reproduction.

Lino and wood cut

Lino and wood cut are both relief printing processes. With wood cutting, the surface of a prepared block of wood is carved with a gouge or chisel tool. Non-printing areas are removed, leaving the printing parts level with the surface. The surface is inked using an ink-covered roller known as a brayer, leaving the printing areas ready to print. Multiple colours can be printed by keying the paper to a frame around the wood blocks.

Linocut images are created in a similar way, by cutting away the base material with a sharp knife or V-shaped chisel or gouge. Both processes work through the transfer of ink from a relief surface on to the substrate.

Both techniques can produce results which have immense atmosphere and unique qualities with every print.

Design is the method of putting form and content together. Design, just as art, has multiple definitions; there is no single definition. Design can be art. Design can be aesthetics. Design is so simple, that's why it is so complicated.

Paul Rand

Porth y Chain ⬅
Sea kayaks at Newgale Beach ⬇
Ian Phillips

These images are produced by reduction, or the 'suicide' method of relief printing. The four colours are cut and printed consecutively from a single piece of lino, starting with the lightest for areas such as the rain and wave tops, and ending with the darkest, usually black, layer. Water-based ink is transferred from lino on to Japanese paper by hand with a Japanese naren.

For looser areas such as the distant hills and the clouds, ink is scrubbed from the block with a damp cloth before printing.

In addition to printing and mark-making methods, students often use other forms of craft-based techniques to explore their design ideas.

Almost any craft-based discipline can be appropriated by graphic design students: ceramics, needlework, or work with other materials such as plaster, metal and wood. These can all lead to the realisation and development of new creative ideas.

Materials

Choosing materials to create the right end result takes a mixture of experience and trial and error. Planning the work from concept through to its final outcome is crucial, but there should always be an allowance for the incidence of the accident, as this could also lead to some startling results.

Testing and exploring materials will not only contribute to the intellectual and physical experience of making something, but will also allow for creative ideas and aesthetic sensibilities to develop. The idea of play and analysis can become key to the final outcome. Technologies such as rapid prototyping or laser cutting (as can be seen with the typographical example on the opposite page), now enable students to create high-quality, resolved work.

By using such techniques and equipment to investigate and conceptualise ideas, remarkable results can be achieved. Until recently, this equipment would have been either unavailable or cost prohibitive to many students and young designers. But as such technologies become cheaper and more readily available within art and design facilities, the range of applications and opportunities has greatly increased.

New Metal Gothic typeface ◒
Kareena Ross-Cumming
(a student at Canterbury College, UK)
The starting point for this typeface was 'Old English Blackletter'. The resulting typeface is presented through laser cutting, out of a single sheet of steel.

Perfect typography is certainly the most elusive of all arts. Sculpture in stone alone comes near it in obstinacy.
Jan Tschichold

Software has evolved greatly since computers were first introduced to design studios in the early 1990s. Computer programs now have the power to manipulate objects or images to an industry or broadcast quality and standard.

Image manipulation

Software programs such as Adobe Photoshop, Adobe Illustrator and Painter allow the designer to explore, manipulate and dramatically edit images using a variety of techniques. This can lead to the creation of highly sophisticated artworks and the production of creative and thought-provoking visuals.

It is important to gain a knowledge and understanding of the processes involved in producing such works. Different software applications can enable the individual to manipulate, retouch, edit, sequence and utilise the digitisation capacities, creating effects that result in a considerable alteration of the original raw data, and sometimes creating a fantastical mirror of reality.

Like all things, technology will continue to evolve, so that both two- and three-dimensional pieces and environments are explored and pushed to the boundaries of perception and iteration. It will continue to create new territories that can amaze and fascinate us.

Summer Triptych ⬆
Dean Samed **(a student at Canterbury Christ Church University, UK)**

This design was created in response to the D&AD Student Awards competition, held in the UK. The brief was to create an unconventional brand campaign for the UK's original pioneer of ethical beauty products, The Body Shop. Dean's work is intended as an invocation of harmony within the natural world. The pieces are a montage of stock images from various sources and have been heavily manipulated in Adobe Photoshop and Corel Painter.

Deconstruct Me ➡
Dean Samed **(a student at Canterbury Christ Church University, UK)**

This self-created piece was part of a series of works created under Dean Samed's alias 'Conzpiracy' on <www.deviantart.com>. The piece was created through heavy retouching and image manipulation.

There are many ways in which an image can be captured and manipulated. The most important part of the image capture process is finding the potential shot and having a strong idea or concept in the first place.

Original analogue images, such as photographs, can of course be reworked through digitisation and manipulation with software applications. Image processing is dependent on the final outcome though: will it be printed, displayed or used online?

Cameras

Cameras come in all shapes, sizes and formats. Digital cameras are becoming increasingly used for image capture and creation purposes. Most of these, including mobile phone cameras, have the capability to deliver high-quality images for print design and screen-based visual communication. Composition is key and the digital camera or capture equipment enables instant feedback and the opportunity to edit and recapture quickly.

Digital cameras and mobile phones ⬇ ⬆
Most digital cameras and mobile phones are able to take photographs in a variety of styles. In the image above, taken on a mobile phone, a setting has been used, mimicking the style of a photograph taken on a Lomo camera (shown below).

 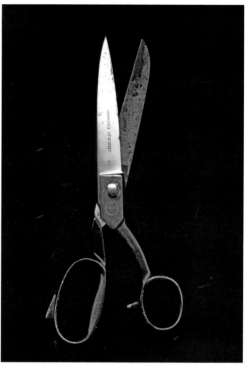

Scanners

Scanners come in various formats: drum, flatbed and film.
Drum scanners still provide the highest quality reproductions
and are used to capture illustration, print making and
analogue photography work. The flatbed scanner is an
inexpensive alternative, and has the capability to create,
capture and digitise anything from a print through to a
sculpture or fragile object. Qualities to consider when
choosing a scanner include optical resolution, optical
density, maximum scanning area and bit-depth outcome.

The results from experimentation (using lo-fi or high-quality
capture devices and equipment), be it accidental or planned,
can be interesting, surprising and creative.

Scanned objects ⬆
These images were created by
scanning actual objects. We generally
think of a scanner as a device for use
with flat artwork, but there is nothing
to prevent experimentation and
modification. Other experiments to
consider include scanning something
that is moving (a clock face for
instance), or altering the position of
the focal plane using a sheet of glass.

Dennis Y Ichiyama

Dennis Y Ichiyama studied and received his Bachelor of Fine Arts degree from the University of Hawaii-Manoa and a Master of Fine Arts in Graphic Design from Yale University, School of Art and Architecture in 1968. Following this, he continued his postgraduate studies in design at the Allgemeine Gewerbeschule, Basel, from 1976 to 1978. He is a practising designer and professor on the Visual Communications Design Programme, at the School of Visual and Performing Arts at Purdue University, USA.

What made you decide to study graphic design?

Growing up in Hawaii, immersed in its beauty and isolation, makes it difficult to seriously consider a profession in design. However, I've been fortunate to have had three outstanding mentors: Kenneth Kingrey (University of Hawaii, 1913–1994), Norman S Ives (Yale, 1923–1978) and Rob Roy Kelly (designer and educator, 1925–2004). They advised, educated and helped me to attain some of my goals.

In your point of view, what are the key things to learn on a course or at college?

Think, plan, organise. The three basic principles I learned at Yale and at the Basel School of Design.

What makes a student successful at college or as a graduate?

Risk taking.

The ability to express oneself (refining writing and speaking skills) and an appreciation of the following quotation:

*'You see things and you say "Why?"
But I dream of things that never were, and I say "Why not?"'*

George Bernard Shaw (1856–1950)

Typeface ➡
Poster designed to promote the documentary film, *Typeface*, directed by Justine Nagan and produced by Kartemquin Films. Printed at the Hamilton Wood Type & Printing Museum in Two Rivers, Wisconsin, US, the eclectic mix of typefaces and the overprinting of forms creates a tactile and dynamic printed piece.

a Kartemquin Films Production

TYPEFACE

Directed & Produced by
Justine Nagan

Executive Producers
Gordon Quinn &
Maria Finitzo

Editor Liz Kaar

Photography Tom Bailey

Associate Producer
Starr Marcello

Sound Zak Piper

design Dennis Y Ichiyama

Rich media is a term used to define media produced using a combination of technologies, including but not limited to sound, video and flash.

Brief

Using an image capturing or multimedia product, in a format that is appropriate to your communication objectives, create a series of images in response to the following. Equipment you might want to consider could include: a mobile phone, a disposable camera, a scanner, a photocopier and a pin-hole camera.

Part one

Create a series of images, photographs or video pieces that correspond to the pairing of the word lists below:

- Tree – shape

- Hair – suite

- Flow – course

- Coat – finish

Part two

Using the work created in part one, produce a 'How to...' guide or instruction manual on the processes you used to achieve your results.

Project objectives

- Development of an experimental approach to new ways of image capturing.

- Exploration of communication strategies.

Recommended reading related to this project

Badger, G. 2007. *The Genius of Photography*. Quadrille Publishing

Napper T. Q. and Monheim, F. 2002. *Lomo: Don't Think, Just Shoot*. Booth-Clibborn Editions

McLuhan, M. and Fiore, Q. 2008. *The Medium is the Massage: An Inventory of Effects*. Penguin Classics

Moggridge, B. 2006. *Designing Interactions*. MIT Press

Rees, D. and Blechman, N. 2008. *How to be an Illustrator*. Laurence King

Chapter 4 – Vocabulary

By developing a suitable design vocabulary, it is possible to convey messages, meaning and information. This section of the book introduces some of the terms we use when articulating our ideas to others, and some of the theories for generating and developing creative work.

Developing a design vocabulary allows for the exploration and investigation of innovative design work. This in turn enables the creation of a variety of design work that can effectively communicate different ideas to an audience.

Cultures, social groups and businesses have their own vocabularies, as do graphic designers. By understanding and embracing this design language, specific approaches to design problems can be communicated and interpreted correctly.

Looking back at history

A developed design vocabulary comes through a process of exploration and investigation and enables messages to be conveyed clearly to both clients and end users.

The specific use of typography, for example, can enhance and clarify meaning. Colouration and style, or evocation of an era or movement, for example, can create a resonance with the audience, thus enabling complicated messages, meaning and information to be embedded and conveyed through the visual outcome.

The careful selection of elements is key to a successful end result. This not only involves the basics such as type, colour, form and scale, but also the quantity and quality of information within the design piece.

Designers have, for many years, looked back through time to historical design pieces. They do this in an attempt to decipher or gain inspiration from such work, and to ask the question, why does it work so well?

The informed design piece can be seen as a collection of design choices and a combination of influences, time zones and cultural metaphors, stemming from a grown and developed vocabulary. This design vocabulary is something that can be easily created by looking widely across many eras, styles and forms of design delivery.

B.O.A.C. (British Overseas Airways) ➔
Beverley Pick

This vibrant and structured piece of design work from the early 1950s has a distinct and powerful visual vernacular.

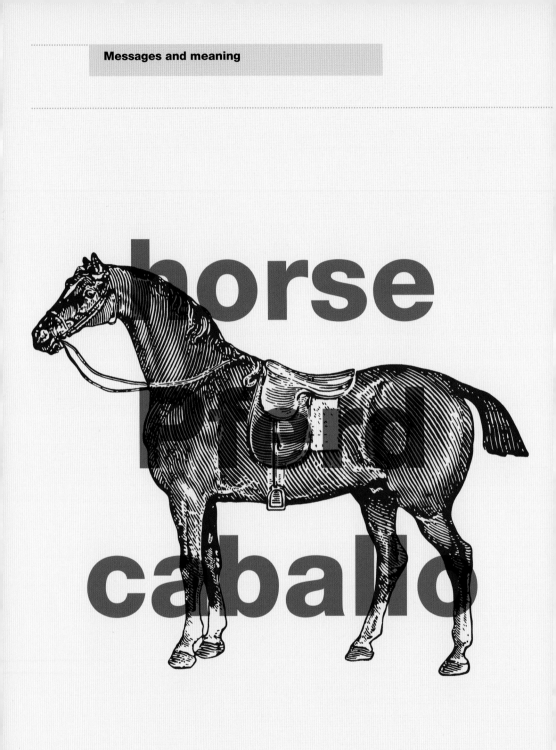

horse
caballo

Messages, meaning and information are quite different from each other. Our recognition of such messages, their meaning and their associations is dependent on our learnt understanding and cultural interpretation, as well as the systems or conventions within which they exist. It is an understanding of this process that underpins much of graphic design.

During the nineteenth century, the American philosopher Charles Sanders Peirce (1839–1914) defined the word 'semiotics' as 'the science of signs'. He believed that signs take the form of words, images, sounds, odours, flavours, acts or objects. However, they essentially have no meaning until a meaning is attributed to them. Similarly, the Swiss linguist Ferdinand de Saussure also proposed that words have no meaning other than that which we give them.

Normally we do not express ourselves by using single linguistic signs, but groups of signs, organised in complexes which themselves are signs.
Ferdinand de Saussure

Signifier and signified

According to Saussure, a sign is constructed from two parts, the 'signified' and the 'signifier'. Only when these two parts come together do we get a 'sign'.

For example, if we take a picture of a horse, this is what is being represented, and could be called the signified. We use the letters H O R S E (each of which are single linguistic signs, representing sounds) to spell the word horse. This word is the signifier, it represents the drawing of the horse. However, this relationship is arbitrary. In German this would be *pferd*, and in Spanish *caballo*. So the relationship between the signified and the signifier is dependent on the context, and our agreed systems or conventions, for example language. This model is often referred to as 'dyadic' (or having two parts).

Say what's on your mind.

Come and talk to one
of our skilled counsellors.

www.leedscounselling.org.uk

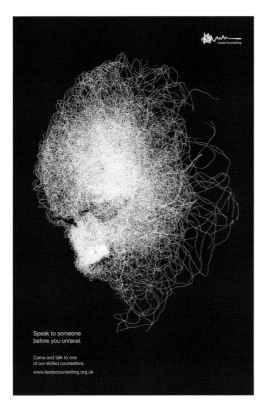

Talking Therapy ◕
Art direction and copy: Richard Irving and Gerard Edmondson at McCann Manchester. Typography: Richard Irving, Jamie Axford, Ryan Alexander. Photography: Steve Deer

Poster promoting the services of Leeds Counselling, an organisation that specialises in the treatment of mental health issues using talking therapies. The individual lines that go to make up the portraits are genuine quotes from clients in counselling sessions. There are twenty quotes in total, repeated ad infinitum in an attempt to signify the turmoil of an unquiet mind. The headlines gently but firmly urge people to open up. Here we can see how the signifiers (the images that are created by the type construct) become a representation of the human being and their mental health issues.

Speak to someone
before you unravel.

Come and talk to one
of our skilled counsellors.
www.leedscounselling.org.uk

What is said determines who listens and who understands. Graphic design is a language, but graphic designers are so busy worrying about the nuances – accents, punctuation and so on – that they spend little time thinking about what the words add up to. I'm interested in using our communication skills to change the way things are.

Tibor Kalman

NAO DIGAS TUDO O QUE PENSAS

PENSA EM TUDO O QUE DIZES

ANTHONY BURRILL FOR TIMELESS: BRITISH COUNCIL & EXD'09 - LISBOA

ANTHONY BURRILL FOR TIMELESS: BRITISH COUNCIL & EXD'09 - LISBOA

Lisbon Posters ⬆
Anthony Burrill

Language is arbitrary. It's a learnt set of understanding.
These posters by Anthony Burrill were part of an
experimental exchange for the British Council /
Experimenta, in Lisbon. Understanding or decoding the
posters requires an understanding of language, which
itself is formed of multiple signifiers (letterforms) that, in
turn, creating meaning.

Peirce also proposed that there were three levels of sign: icon, index and symbol, in terms of how they denote their objects.

Icon

Any sign that physically resembles (whether through sight, sound, smell, touch or taste) the thing that it represents could be described as an icon. For example, a photograph of someone could be described as an iconic sign, in that it physically resembles the person that it represents. In graphic design, icons can be reduced to their simplest form. This technique is employed in pictograms, such as those used to distinguish gender on the signs of public toilets.

Index

An index has a direct link between the sign and the object. A street sign, for example, only makes sense by its precise placement in the street. When placed at the end of a road or junction, a stop sign gives a clear instruction to a driver. We understand the sign, but we only really understand the instruction in relation to its placement.

Symbol

A symbol bears no logical resemblance to the thing it depicts. The relationship between the object and sign must be learned in order to understand its representation. National flags or logos that represent a company or organisation are examples of symbols. So too are alphabets, punctuation and Morse code. The swastika, for example, is an ancient symbol of life and good luck. However, it was adopted by the Nazi Party in 1920 and for many it still represents hatred, anti-Semitism, violence, death and murder. Unlike an index sign, it represents this irrespective of placement.

Alice's Adventures in Wonderland ➡
***Alexandra Bucktin* (a student at Leeds College of Art)**

Created in response to the 2010 Puffin Children's Design Award brief, this design evokes many of the themes found in the story *Alice's Adventures in Wonderland*. The group of icons (the teapot and the hare, for example) make the shape of a heart, a signifier of the experiences that Alice had during her adventures.

ALICE'S ADVENTURES IN WONDERLAND

LEWIS CARROLL

Graphic design is about the visual display of specific messages for an intended audience. Central to this is the meaning held by, and attributed to, the various visual elements, for example text, images and illustrations. Here, we will examine some of the ways in which this meaning is assigned and developed.

Encoding and decoding

Is there such a thing as an uncoded message within visual communication? Amongst semioticians, the answer is likely to be 'no'. They believe that everything is pre-encoded, and that this encoding comes from experiences that have been mapped by the human brain. We understand what we see through these experiences and do not consciously question the values or inherent meanings held within. Our 'decoding' comes through interpretation and evaluation, by relating the value of the meaning to its relevant coding.

Implication through text and image or the combination of the two leads to what is 'meant' being more important than 'what is said'. We respond to a process of 'transmission', where a sender (voice) transmits the communication to the receiver (audience) so that meaning becomes 'content'.

Dark Love

Design: Propaganda
Photography: James Stroud
This photography project for make-up brand Illamasqua, focuses on the alter-egos of regular gothic, burlesque and fetish party-goers. The provocative and secretive nature of the project is not explicitly 'said' but is instead subtly 'encoded' through a use of foils, ornate typefaces, minimal text intervention and a half dust-jacket outer.

No religion. All faith.

Denotation – what is pictured?

Any element, be it text or image, exists on two distinct levels of meaning: its denotive level, and its connotative level.

Denotation refers to physicality, in that if we view an object or subject which is not the real thing – a photograph or an illustration, for example – we are viewing the object or subject as a representation of itself. So if it was, say, an image of a dog, the image we are viewing is only a representation of 'dogs'. This is what is known in semiotics as 'signification'. Even when the image of the dog sits alongside a range of images of different dogs, the meaning will be the same: 'dog'.

Connotation – how is it pictured?

This is the second level of signification, as recognised by Roland Barthes. The fact that we all experience different cultures means that the reading of an image is affected by individual and group viewpoints. This happens to such an extent that our understanding of information and meaning can be attributed to a combination of knowledge, learning and experience gained throughout life. This combination of learning and experience determines our perception of all meaning within any given image or circumstance. Therefore, the 'connotation' of an image is relative and dependent on our cultural relationships. The reading of the image is therefore arbitrary, in that we conjure the meaning through these learnt rules as we develop throughout life.

As designers we need to consider firstly what we are saying, and secondly how we are saying it. When we speak, we not only say words and sentences, we also have a tone of voice. Images and typography are no different. In the dog example, there are not only hundreds of types of dogs, there are also many ways of representing the image. A photograph of a Rottweiler for instance, on one level is a dog, but how that image is presented will affect our reading of it. For example, a halftone image may imply it is from a newspaper, while a watercolour illustration may imply a family portrait.

What is said
HOW IT IS SAID

WORKSHOP A

ワークショップ エー

793-0003　愛媛県西条市西ひうち6-8
TEL：0897-56-1108
FAX：0897-55-7751

blue f*ield

www.blue-field.com

Presenting visual imagery

There are various other ways in which photographic images can be included and used when constructing a design piece. The communication of the final design piece is dependent on the reading of the image, in relation to any text contained within the piece or through the presentation of the meaning constructed within it.

Careful choice and selection of all imagery is crucial, along with a consideration and approach to the value of the visual communication.

Type and image: When imagery is added to the typographic construct, the resulting outcome can often result in extra meaning and messages. Experiments in the usage of images within the design piece will also provide the designer with a greater understanding of how meaning can be formed.

Juxtaposition: This is when multiple images are placed in close proximity to one another. Juxtaposition can be a useful way of drawing the viewer's attention to objects, images or image and text that are in opposition to each other. It can be a useful way of proposing comparison or contrast.

Superimposition: Superimposition refers to the placing or layering of one image over another. This approach is typically used to add to the overall image effect, but can also sometimes be used to conceal something.

Montage: Montage involves combining an image or images to make a single composite through the process of cutting and/or joining a number of other images together.

Intervention: The intervention and interaction of images with each other or other objects.

Workshop A poster, Blue Field ◖
Nigel Aono-Billson

This poster was produced to promote an exhibition of work for a pan-European/Japanese textile designer/maker at Workshop A, in Saijo, Japan. Careful placement of text and image gives greater meaning to the design, which reflects the philosophy of the workshop and the work carried out there.

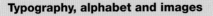

THE HISSING SOUND OF A TAPE PLAYER

The term 'typography' comes from the study of typefaces and their systematic classification. Each typeface is a family of letters corresponding to the alphabet and which, generally speaking, also includes numerals and punctuation.

The study of typography is used as a means to introduce typefaces and the study of classical and contemporary typographic design. Through this study, we can begin to understand how typography can convey messages with meaning.

Again, when working with type, it is crucial to consider the configuration of the construct or form through shape, structure, balance and hierarchy. By doing this, the message can be conveyed to the audience as desired.

The best way to gain a good understanding and grounding in the usage of type within graphic design is through a series of typographical exercises. These act as an introduction to the appreciation and understanding of all the fundamental conventions and functions of typography. These exercises should cover typographical territory, such as composition and layout, hierarchy and balance, grids and structure, proportions and spacing, alignment and type anatomy.

'Inngarsol' typeface ⟵ ⬇
***Robert Kennett* (a student at Canterbury College, UK)**

The 'hissing sound of a tape player' inspired the creation of this unique typeface, which explores the expressive potential of letterforms. The typeface challenges the reader with its use of proportions, scale and legibility.

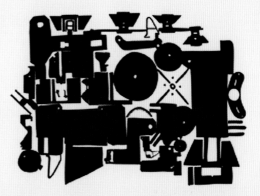

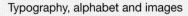

The homeless shelter project ⬆ ➡
Katie Fetchtmann **(a student at ESAG
Penninghen, France)**

This project uses recycled movie and
advertising posters to make summer shelters
for the homeless population of Paris. Each
completed modular shelter measures two
metres by two metres. A typographical
exploration of form results in a typeface
('Paper Font', right) derived from the folding
of printed sheets.

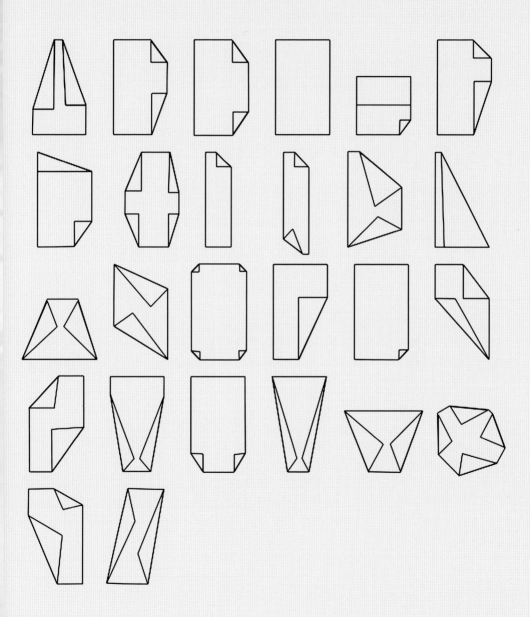

The origins of the printed word date back to the fifteenth century and the invention of Gutenberg's printing press. The invention and establishment of this printing press started the process of the transference of printed words on to paper.

Historical type classification

As with drawing, the learning and consideration of proportions through scale and form are important considerations when we come to type and all its applications. Type recognition, the understanding of typography and the ability to use it well, is an essential requirement for all graphic designers.

Historically, it has been suggested that the origins of type can be traced as far back as the Minoan civilisation in Greece, between 1850 BC and 1600 BC. Movable typefaces are believed to have originated in China during the eleventh century and modular metal type some time later in Korea, in 1230. Therefore, type existed in its rawest form some centuries before the invention of the Gutenberg press.

Typefaces can be classified in numerous ways, but they are commonly separated into three main categories: old style, transitional and modern. These classifications relate directly to when a style or cut was first seen or who the typeface was designed by.

As with many things, there is a great deal of discussion and disagreement when it comes to the subject of type. It is important for designers to familiarise themselves with the common themes and theories so as to gain a comprehensive understanding of the subject.

Further classification

There are many ways in which type can be classified. A historical and practical classification of type aids the designer to more accurately access and select a typeface to work well with a particular design piece.

Some classification methods group typefaces purely on the individual character parts or their shape (and not their history), so a knowledge of the anatomy of type can also allow the designer to classify a variety of unfamiliar fonts.

Having an understanding of 'good typography' is an essential means for a designer to give voice to the visual idea, and to its shape and form. Through this understanding, it is possible to produce creative work that has a natural harmony and balance.

Different typefaces tell different stories. They are more than simply shapes representing sounds; they also come with historical and cultural baggage that needs to be understood in order to be exploited.

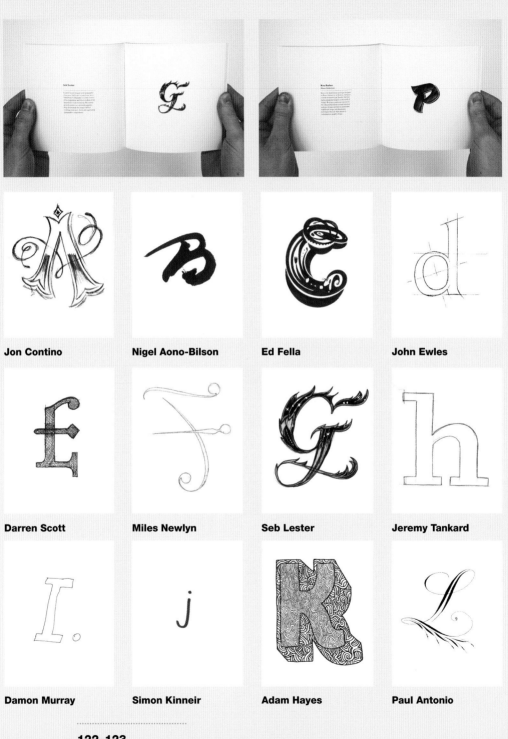

Jon Contino

Nigel Aono-Bilson

Ed Fella

John Ewles

Darren Scott

Miles Newlyn

Seb Lester

Jeremy Tankard

Damon Murray

Simon Kinneir

Adam Hayes

Paul Antonio

Ken Garland

James Le Beau-Morley

Maxwell Lord

Ken Barber

Lida Lopes Cardozo.

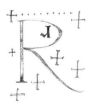

Jonathan Barnbrook

Simon Spilsbury

Bruce Duckworth

Peter Saville

Veronika Burian

Alison Carmichael

Rian Hughes

Stephen Banham

Alan Ariail

Characters – an eclectic alphabet
Will Foley **(a student at the University of Gloucestershire, UK)**

For this project, each character was specially commissioned from a leading typographer, type designer or creative working with type as part of their core creative practice. The resulting book (shown top left) is an eclectic and exotic mix of typographic visions.

An understanding of the principles of space, balance and hierarchy within creative practices such as architecture, fine art and industrial design, is core to the production of good design. When applied to all the elements on a page they form the basis of a graphic designer's 'design vocabulary'.

As well as being pivotal to the creation of good design, these principles are also fundamental to all composition, leading to intentional and decisive conclusions.

White space is the lungs of the layout. It's not there for aesthetic reasons. It's there for physical reasons.
Derek Birdsall

Space

Space is the context within which all design elements exist: a physical environment where a message is formed and perceived. In terms of layout or when we come to the page, it is bound by the edges of the page. This frame, created or physical, defines the area of activity and acts as a boundary within which spatial context occurs. This context differs from the base or ground due to the fact that we do not have a front/back relationship. The context is therefore alluded to by the edge/boundary of the active/worked area. A front/back relationship may be suggested by the existence of the edge/boundary. Despite this, both spatial context and figure/ground can reside alongside each other.

White space

The term 'white space' or 'negative space' refers to the space between and around all the design elements, such as the text and images, the margins and gutters, along with the space between columns of text and between the lines of type. It derives its name from the white paper that is visible.

The correct use of white space can add an elegance to the form and structure of the layout, and can enhance the rhythmical qualities of the design.

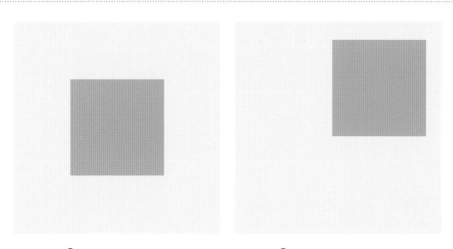

Passive ⬆

The white space in this symmetrical layout is passive: it is only the background for the central element to stand on. The margins or border are therefore passive and are not key to the reading of the layout.

Active ⬆

An asymmetrical layout suggests motion and activity. This is due to the unequal order and balance of the elements, making a dynamic layout. The white space here is no longer passive and informs us of the dynamism of the layout.

Recessive ⬆

Here the dominant element is the perimeter (white space) around the central element. The space becomes the positive shape in this arrangement.

Dominant ⬆

Here the element becomes the main focus of attention.

Balance

When creating a design, it is crucial that the individual elements have a harmonious balance. To be well balanced, the design must have a clear and concise message. It has been suggested that there are possibly three main states of balance: symmetry, asymmetry and static or noise.

A symmetrical design is vertical and centrally balanced. These are often more formal in their context and usage. Asymmetrical designs are less rigid and are generally more varied with the use of their content. Static or noise designs are those that are either deliberately chaotic or poorly considered, or of limited legibility.

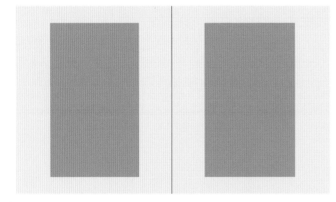

Symmetrical
In a symmetrical layout, verso and recto (left- and right-hand) pages are mirror images of one another. This presents a calm and balanced arrangement.

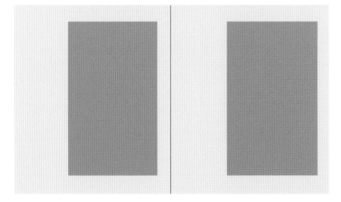

Asymmetrical
In an asymmetrical layout the verso and recto pages are the same, as opposed to the symmetrical grid seen before. This creates a more dynamic and active arrangement, as the eye is drawn across the page. This also introduces different width margins, again adding dynamism.

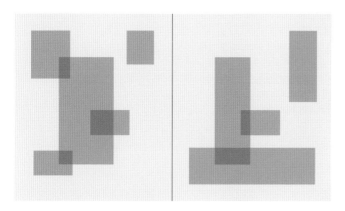

Static or noise
Noise is a chaotic or poorly considered layout or arrangement.

In addition to these main three states, there are also some general 'rules' that can be used when creating compositions:

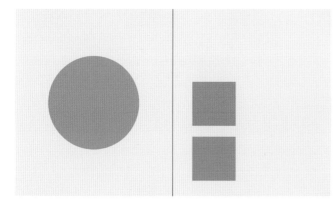

Rule of odds
The rule of odds states that a viewer generally finds it more comfortable to see a composition that contains an odd number of elements. This is usually formed by having the central item, in this case a circle, 'framed' by an even number of supporting elements, in this case two squares.

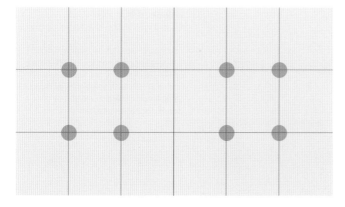

Rule of thirds
The rule of thirds is a technique common in photography and art. By dividing the page into thirds, you effectively create 'hot spots' of interest and focus. This also encourages the placement of objects off-centre, adding dynamism to the page.

Hierarchy

By establishing a hierarchy of elements, we can express the importance of each element. There are various ways in which we can achieve this hierarchy: by grouping, by colour or by commonality, for example. This helps the audience to read the design and thus facilitates the delivery of the content or message.

Each design piece should contain a strong focal point to draw the eye of the viewer or audience around the design.

There are many ways of adding a hierarchy, some of which are shown here.

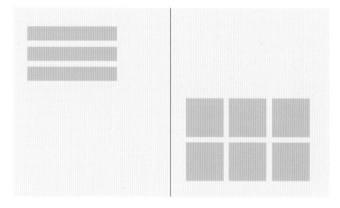

Grouping
The thoughtful grouping of elements together in a layout will aid expression and give importance to certain elements. Using size as one of the hierarchies can add to this, giving emphasis when needed.

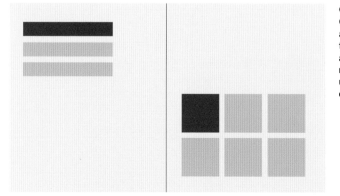

Colour
Colour adds a hierarchical value to a layout, as well as providing contrast to the main text. It is often used for a purpose or a strategy or to aid the reader/viewer, but not to confuse them unless it is a deliberate part of the design.

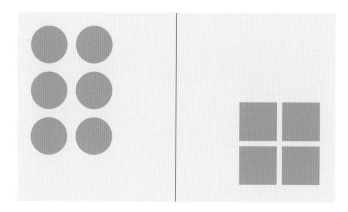

Commonality ⟵
Shape, scale and alignment lead to harmony within the structure of a layout. By grouping similar elements, through colour and commonality, content can be organised with a focus on the delivery.

In addition to these main three hierarchies you may also consider:

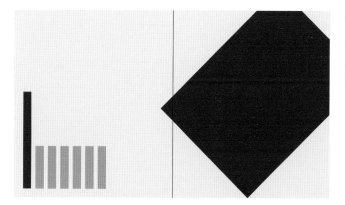

Orientation ⟵
Never assume that images and text should be placed straight. Experiment with aligning vertically, sometimes called 'broadside', or by placing elements on angles and varying orientations.

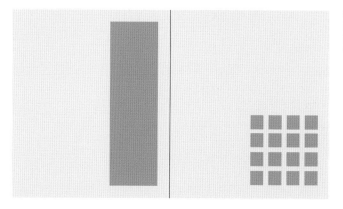

Scale ⟵
Experimenting with scale can introduce a hierarchy and can control the reader's flow.

Works
Propaganda

This self-promotion piece features a strong sense of hierarchy, using varying scales of typography, multiple orientations and calm and considered placement of imagery. The red A2 screen-printed box contains a series of posters showcasing the design agency's capabilities.

An understanding of how images and text work in layout underpins much graphic design teaching. The way in which the layout is composed can add value and enhance the text with feeling or attitude. This can affect the very way in which it is read, viewed or even perceived.

Creating a layout does not only concern the placement of text on a page, but also the way in which it works with the integration of images or the other page elements. With design for print (such as for brochures, books, journals, annual reports and branding), much of the basis for layout is derived from aesthetic values; traditionally, good layout should guide the reader through the text. Ultimately, the final object or product will have a determination on the layout – the content very much has a handle on the form. So, different books need to be treated in different ways, as do magazines and newspapers, websites and three-dimensional forms, such as packaging or wayfinding and information systems.

Basic principles

The golden section and golden ratio are a classical or formal way of producing a composition and construction with a harmonious balance. These 'divine proportions' hold a fascination for many designers, particularly in the creation of grids for layout and page formats.

The golden section and golden ratio is the bisection of a line at a point, using the mathematical equation: a: b = b: (a+b) or equation: (Phi) ϕ = 1.618033988749895...

This equation can also be seen in the numerical sequence called the Fibonacci sequence. Each number in this sequence is the sum of the two preceding numbers. By dividing the value of the preceding numbers, the result is a proportional scaling, equal to that of the golden section.

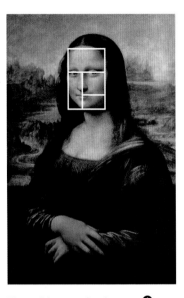

The golden section in art

Within Leonardo da Vinci's painting, The Mona Lisa, there lies a myriad of golden rectangles. This is especially evident in the construction of the subject's face.

0, 1, 1, 2, 3, 5, 8, 13, 21, 34, 55, 89, 144, 233, 377, 610, 987, 1597, 2584, 4181, 6765...

Fibonacci's numbers
The first 20 numbers in the Fibonacci sequence (also written as Fn). Each number is the sum of the two preceding numbers. These give proportions that frequently appear in art and design.

Creating a symmetrical grid
Use the golden rectangle to create a symmetrical grid and layout.

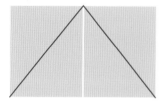

1
Take two equal, proportioned pages. Create half-diagonal lines from the centre to the bottom left (verso) and right (recto) corners of each page.

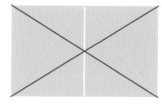

2
Create a full diagonal line from the centre to the bottom left (verso) and right (recto) corners of each page.

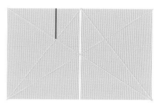

3
Draw a line from the intersection of the half-diagonal and full-diagonal lines on the left (verso) page, to the top of the page.

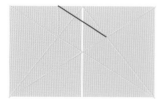

4
Draw a line from the point at the top or head of the left (verso) page back across to the intersection point of the half-diagonal and full-diagonal lines on the right (recto) page.

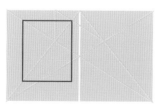

5
Draw a line from the new intersection on the half-diagonal line on the left (verso) page, to the left to link with the full-diagonal line, then downward to intersect with the half-diagonal line, back across and up to create an area where the text will sit.

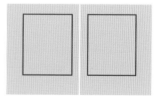

6
Repeat the same steps but this time on the right (recto) page. This will give you two fully balanced, symmetrical areas for text creation.

Learning the rules

By creating a structure, or 'grid', using vertical and horizontal coordinates, a designer can experiment with the placement of content at various positions on the page. The grid determines where content can appear and it is the basis for construction – a tool or framework where text and images can be ordered.

Grids can be symmetrical, asymmetrical or modular and can be as simple or as complex as the design requires.

Layout requires consideration in application and usage. It is also an important factor to be considered in the creation of wayfinding and information systems, along with other 3D usage such as on packaging design and labels.

Breaking the rules (deconstruction)

'There is nothing outside the text', stated Jacques Derrida, the postmodernist French philosopher, when he first introduced the proposition of 'deconstruction'. Derrida not only suggested that text could have more than one meaning, he also suggested that it could, in fact, contain several irreconcilable and contradictory meanings. In other words, beneath the text there lies a subtext or set of values that can also be evaluated, but without meaning and in contradiction to the text.

Deconstruction is a complex notion; meaning needs a context but because context is constantly in flux, meaning becomes indeterminate. By breaking the rules of the formalised grid, the layout can no longer be considered in the same way.

The deconstruction of text and its elements is a cause for revision and re-reading. This involves breaking down all the design parts into their constituents, before rethinking the ways in which the work can be read or interpreted.

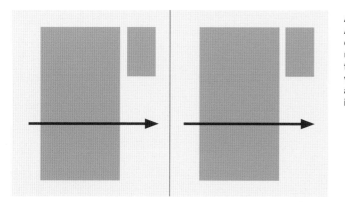

Asymmetrical grid

An asymmetrical layout with two columns. The recto and verso pages use the same grid, as opposed to the symmetrical grid seen below. The wider column contains the core text and the thinner column could contain information, captions or instructions.

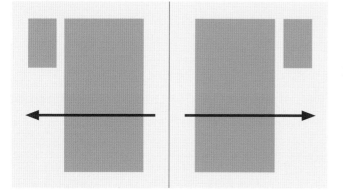

Symmetrical grid

This layout shows a two-column symmetrical grid: recto and verso pages are mirrored, demonstrating a balanced but predictable layout. Again, the wider column contains the core text and the thinner column could contain information, captions or instructions.

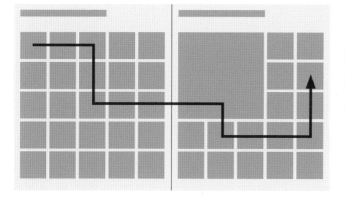

Modular grid

The modular grid is constructed using a series of blocks or modules. A module-based grid can be either symmetrical or asymmetrical in construction (as shown above). Another facet of this grid structure is that elements, for example images, can span multiple modules.

Less

Design

The world is crowded with techniques for getting ideas to stick and be memorable. Without debating the merits of all of them, let's just say that we have one of our own.

Simplicity in design, simplicity in messaging. As the influential designer Dieter Rams said, "Less but better." Enough said.

Rodeo Mailer
Rodeo

This self-promotional mailer makes creative use of space, balance and hierarchy within a grid. All items are carefully placed, creating a sense of pace and dynamism, whilst retaining a clear epression of hierarchy. The grid is both 'used' and 'broken', with text bleeding off the perimeter of the page.

Studio interview:

Wout de Vringer

Wout de Vringer started his studies in graphic design at the Academie voor Künst en Vormgeving Den Bosch in 1979. He now runs his own studio in The Hague with fellow designer Ben Faydherbe.

Did you have any design/creative influence(s) that inspired you during your studies?

I really liked the work from Hard Werken at the time. Their work was bold, colourful, fresh and different from anything you learned at the academy and therefore I found it very attractive. I also liked some of the work from Studio Dumbar. Back then, that was also totally different from all the Swiss-based design that was everywhere.

In hindsight, the work I was 'rebelling' against has had a much bigger influence on my career than the work I admired back then!

Did you do a placement and was it useful to your study experience?

I did and it was very helpful for me. Before, my work was sometimes going in too many different directions and through my internship I learned to focus more on just one. And I also learned how to make a good professional presentation and be able to explain the work to people.

Before, my presentations sometimes were a bit sloppy. Not intentionally – just because I didn't know any better! You have to remember it was the pre-computer era, so everything had to be done by hand: cutting out type, pasting, making drawings, cutting out images or homemade photos and assembling them together to make the presentation. To make that look good is difficult and that's one important thing I learned during my internships. As a result, my final year presentation looked awesome at the degree show! I even won the graphic design department prize of the academy (my only prize ever, unfortunately).

What was the most important aspect of the course for you?

Learning how to communicate with an audience through my work. And learning that having fewer ideas in one project is much better than having too many. In the beginning, I was adding too many ideas in to a single project and even though they were often good ideas it didn't work because it became confusing and therefore my work wasn't communicating.

What makes a student successful at college or as a graduate?

A student who is flexible and willing to accept criticism, but also investigative and sometimes a little bit stubborn – someone who doesn't give up easily!

Today, we can convert any design or sketch work of a letterform into a typeface. By examining the existing different categories, and by thinking about the progress made in printing, imaging and visual communication, new forms can be created for visual communication design work.

Brief

Design and present a typeface design in response to one of the following themes or starting points.

Part one

Pick a theme from the list below:

- Mechanics

- Analogue

- Sequence

Design and draw the letters A–Z in either upper or lower case and the numerals 1–9. The inclusion of punctuation is optional. Consider a title or name from the early stages of the project as this may become the name for your typeface.

Take an experimental approach to design ideas and investigate contemporary and non-traditional approaches to this area of design.

Part two

Decide on a suitable method or mechanical way of completing and finishing your design work. Then produce a poster to promote the typeface.

Project objectives

- Investigation of approaches to contemporary and non-traditional design.

- Experimentation with design ideas.

- Creation of a poster-sized design piece.

Recommended reading related to this project

Carson, D. and L. Blackwell, L. 1995. *The End of Print: The Graphic Design of David Carson*. Chronicle Books

Herbert, S. 2004. *Pioneers of Modern Typography*. Lund Humphries Publishers Ltd

Kane, J. 2002. *A Type Primer*. Laurence King

Tschichold, J. 2006. *The New Typography, Weimar and Now: German Cultural Criticism*. University of California Press

VanderLans , R., Licko, Z., Gray, M. E. and Keedy, J. 1994. *Emigre (The Book): Graphic Design into the Digital Realm*. John Wiley & Sons Inc

Weingart, W. 1999. *Weingart: Typography - My Way to Typography: Retrospective in Ten Chapters*. Lars Muller Publishers

Chapter 5 – Responses

Experimenting with typography and image, in the context of practice, brings new challenges that can lead on to alternative creative solutions in practice.

This section explores how, as designers, we can develop creative responses to the design brief. We look at testing, prototyping and the presentation of design work.

All design problems can be broken down into a number of elements or parts which, when pulled together, ultimately amount to a final design outcome.

To achieve a clear and evolved solution, the starting point must begin with idea generation. Through this process, we can develop ways to creatively originate and conceive of our ideas and produce suitable solutions to the design problem, which will lead to the production of a successful and considered communicative conclusion.

Responding to a brief

The starting point for any design work comes with the assignment or creative brief. This is usually devised by a client or commissioner, and will inform the designer of the task or problem that requires a creative response.

The brief will generally stipulate the type of output or requirements needed, but not always. This forms the basis for initial research and inquiry, and identifies the possible directions that the creativity may take and therefore the starting point for the creative process.

Responses and investigation

When a brief is not supplied, it will be necessary to create one. Creating a brief along with a proposal for working may be a requirement of a study programme or a client or commissioner.

In the case of the client or commissioner, notes would need to be taken during a meeting or briefing. These notes will form the basis of the creative brief and a formal structure for discussion and approval. Accuracy and detail is key to promoting a set of foundations from which to work.

Once agreement has been met with the client, commissioner or even tutor, work may begin. Remember that the brief should accurately reflect all the aims and objectives to be met and taken forward by the design project.

Research and idea creation can then take place, with design development, testing and, ultimately, implementation of the final design solution.

Responding to a brief ➡
There are many alternative approaches that can be taken by a designer to respond to the creative problem. This diagram is a simple overview of some of the stages that are involved in answering the brief. They form building blocks or a direction that will inform the development and production of the creative outcome.

1 **Idea generation and mapping**

Where does your idea come from – how are you going to 'chart' your ideas evolution?

2 **Exploring and investigating**

How are you going to develop your idea?

3 **Communicating your ideas**

How are you going to communicate your ideas to peers and clients?

4 **Developing a design language**

What will influence your design, both in context and appearance?

5 **Understanding messages**

What do the elements you use mean? Are you in control of images and text?

6 **Generating responses**

What will it look like? What form will it take?

7 **Producing your design**

How will you turn an idea into a working prototype?

8 **Testing your outcomes**

Did your idea work? How do you evaluate success? Did it answer the brief?

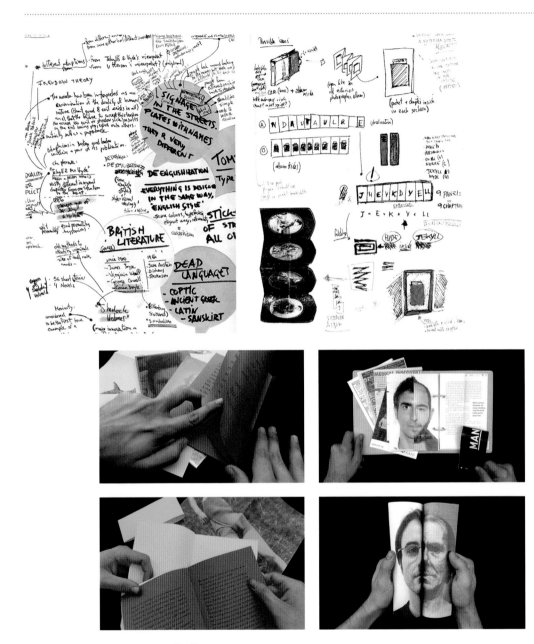

Hybrid Book ⬆ ➔
Alberto Hernández (a student at London College of Communication, UK)

This book deals with the conveyance of layers of information and meaning through a series of visual outcomes. The design language is developed through sketch work (top) early tests and development (above), culminating in the final outcome (opposite).

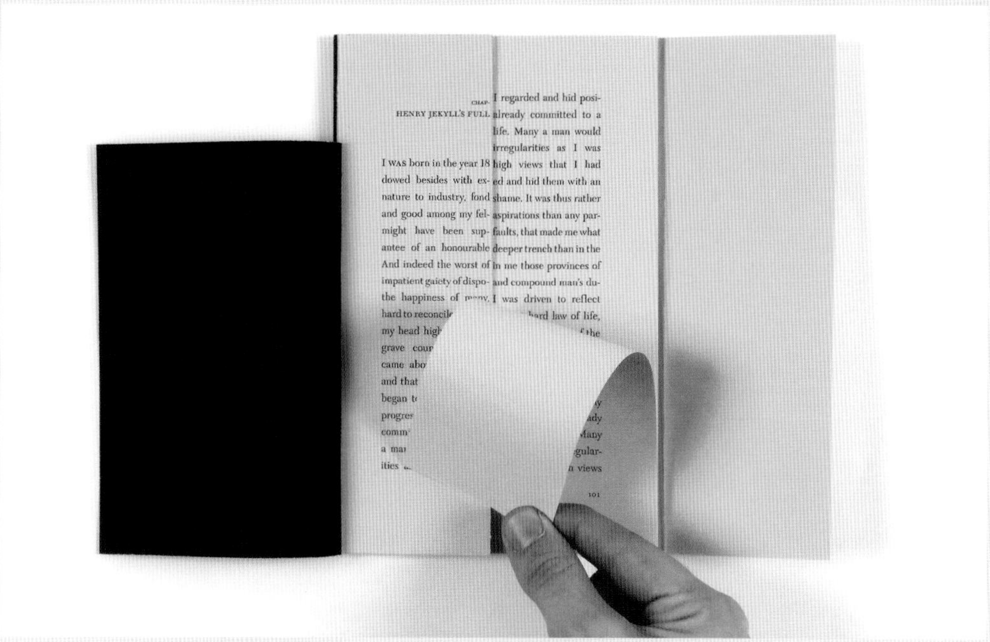
CHAP-
HENRY JEKYLL'S FULL
I WAS born in the year 18
dowed besides with ex-
nature to industry, fond
and good among my fel-
might have been sup-
antee of an honourable
And indeed the worst of
impatient gaiety of dispo-
the happiness of many,
I regarded and hid posi-
already committed to a
life. Many a man would
irregularities as I was
high views that I had
ed and hid them with an
shame. It was thus rather
aspirations than any par-
faults, that made me what
deeper trench than in the
in me those provinces of
and compound man's du-
I was driven to reflect
101

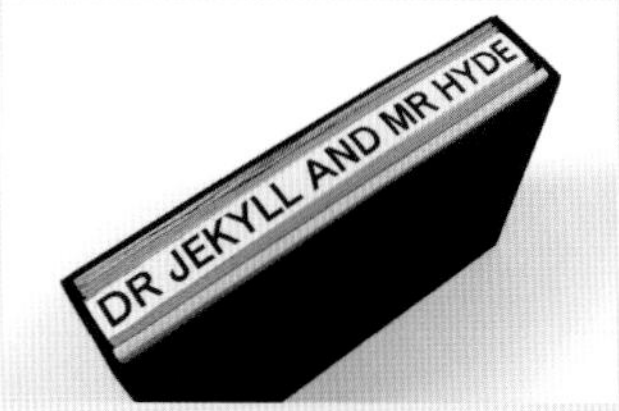
DR JEKYLL AND MR HYDE

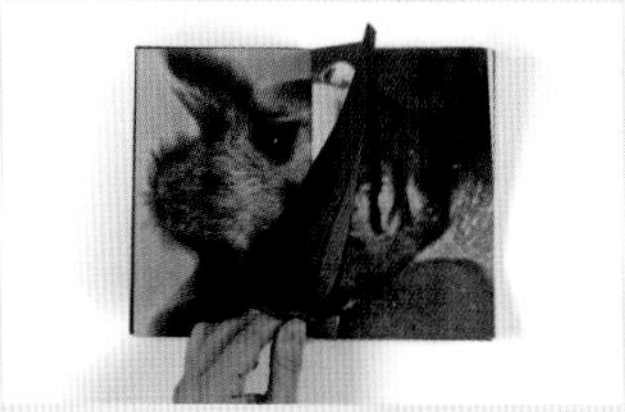

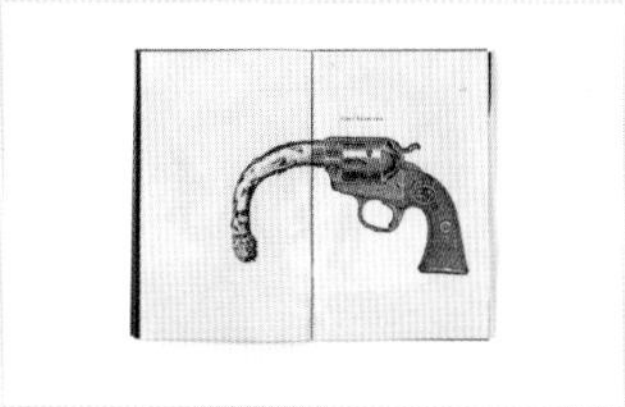

Fat Men!
BRANDY
ILLNESS
MARTELL

DR JEKYLL AND MR HYDE

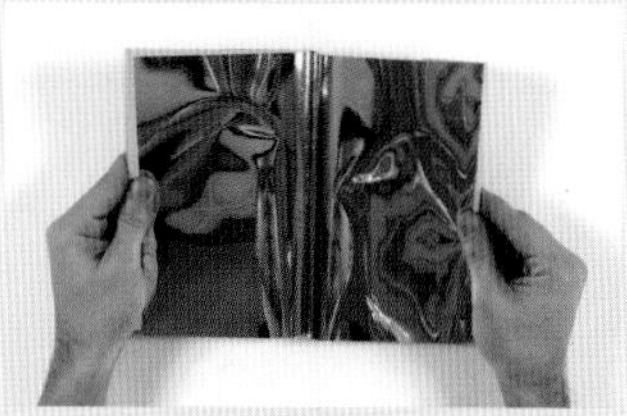

Where do creative ideas and solutions come from? A variety of methods are used to generate multiple ideas. All of these come in direct response to an assignment given by a client or brief. The clues are there to puzzle with and if we try to approach the problem in a calculated manner, the result should usually manifest itself without too much pain.

That enlightened moment when we recognise the answer, that 'epiphany' or 'eureka' moment, has been discussed and explored by theorists and psychologists for many years. For many, this is a 'feeling', a 'gut instinct', and finding the solution to the design problem ultimately comes down to intuition.

Unconscious ideas

Our unconscious has a way of manifesting answers. By storing and processing all the different influences and stimuli we gather along the way, our unconscious can often lead to a solution or series of possible solutions. Experimenting with materials can lead to a creative outpouring of these solutions.

But sometimes, designers find their ideas 'block' and they struggle to find solutions to the design problem. This can be helped by simply taking a break and leaving the project for a while. Focusing on something else and talking to others about the project and the problem and trying to get another perspective on it, can all be enormously helpful. The block may be simply due to the pressure being experienced in finding the right solution. Often, the more we struggle, the harder it becomes to provide a responsive or suitable solution. Teamwork, peer review and creative support and direction will all aid the solution and break the blockage.

Above all, it is vital to experiment with alternative solutions: trying different approaches and methods, sketching, image creating, and exploring materials can all lead to new ideas and solutions. It is also important at this stage to ensure that all work is saved – remember that going back through earlier design ideas can help to develop the concept further.

Peace or Piece ⬅ ⬇
Benjamin Edwards (a student at The University of Derby, UK)
These posters form part of a visual identity aimed at promoting awareness of the issues surrounding gun culture amongst youngsters in urban areas. The result is an evocative design, effective in attracting the attention of its audience.

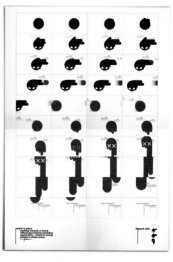

Parker Jotter Anniversary Desk ⬆
Billie Jean

Celebrating 50 years of the Parker Jotter pen, Parker and Pentagram
commissioned Billie Jean to produce this piece of work. It was apparently
inspired by Billie Jean's memory of being bought a Parker pen by his parents
as an initiation into adulthood, and his subsequent use of it to pick the wax
from his ears and deface his school desk!

Nicolas Sarkozy's diary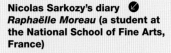
Raphaëlle Moreau (a student at
the National School of Fine Arts,
France)

These two visual representations
of the diary of the French president
demonstrate the creative display
of information. The solid black
bars denote time when there is no
information about the president's
movements – creating a 'map' of
movements over a period of time.

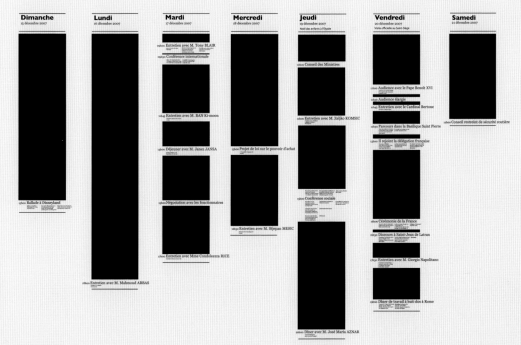

Typographic responses

Using type is one of the most basic challenges that a designer will have to meet. Selecting type is a sensitive exercise requiring an understanding of the role and function of each selected typeface, its characteristics, communicative qualities and its appropriateness.

Misuse of a typeface can confuse an audience or viewer – sometimes to such an extent that the message can be completely lost. Some typefaces are purely to be used for display, while others are for headline or body copy. Type on its own can also create its own image or picture. The shapes and spaces inhabited by type interact with one another and so can become pure form in their own right.

Type can also be non-traditional, hand-drawn or even accidental and undesigned. Examples of this can frequently be found on architecture, shop fascias and signage all over the world. As we have already seen, a thorough understanding of typography and the anatomy and history of type is essential in order for an effective response to the design brief to be formulated.

Pleasure ⬅
Ben Rix **(a student at Brighton University, UK)**

A self-initiated project celebrating the rich cultural references and styles of vintage glamour magazines, using illustration and experimentation in typography and image making.

Everyday items ⬆
Sara Yates **(a student at Leeds College of Art, UK)**

A self-initiated brief, involving the usage and application of typography and its terms. By using the categories of work, eat and sleep, a set of designs was developed to enforce the importance of typographic understanding in daily life.

There are three responses to a piece of design:
'Yes', 'No' and 'WOW!' 'Wow' is the one to aim for.
Milton Glaser

What the World Needs Now ⬆
Billie Jean

An anti-Iraq War poster. The use of vibrant colours and hand-lettered type gives this piece an overriding sense of immediacy. However, it also harks back to 1960s peace and love, hippiesque visual metaphors, now so established in the design-world psyche.

Hand Rendered ⬅
Billie Jean

This design is a celebration of the art of hand lettering in this digital age. It describes the immediacies of idea and concept creation. But it has a personal touch, rich with its own importance and individuality.

Visual research

Creating a series of visual reference sheets or boards (or mood boards), encompassing all the research so far, will help to support the idea creation stage. These could be as simple as a scrapbook-type assemblage of magazine cuttings, 'doodlings' and print-outs from the Internet. These explorations will help to build a picture of the subject, criteria, location and user profile. From a marketing perspective, they will also help in identifying competition or similar product service offerings.

Further development of ideas through sketch work (not directly onto a computer), or test pieces will lead to a greater understanding of your creative ideas and will allow you to measure how appropriate your ideas have been in response to the client brief.

Mock-ups

The production of physical pieces in the form of mock-ups is a regular requirement to demonstrate application, form and structure. It is crucial for the concept and idea to be appropriate or 'Fit for Purpose', and creating mock-ups might help to flag up a number of issues, including:

1. Does the object work in three-dimensions? Proof check it, on the pack or mock-up.

2. Where and how will the finished design piece be seen? Print it out and place it on the wall to see how it looks in reality.

3. Computer screens are not accurate in terms of actual scale. Always print out and proof check design work for accuracy and scale.

4. Colours look different on screen to in print. Print it out and check against a colour system chart.

Barkly's ➡
Lindsey Faye Sherman **(a student at Maryland Institute College of Art, Baltimore, USA)**

This packaging for Barkly's dog treats was designed with the discerning shopper in mind. With a focus on sensory experience, through bold imagery and appetising flavours, the packaging has a distinctive formula.

Products and services are constantly tested to check that they are focused or orientated correctly for acceptance by the consumer and end user. To check this, marketeers use focused testing methods in the form of market research or similarly based mechanisms.

Design is a plan for arranging elements in such a way as best to accomplish a particular purpose.
Charles Eames

Market testing

Market testing, focus groups, user testing and strategic thinking all come under the banner of marketing.

During the research stages of a design project, a designer or design company will usually engage in an audit or will trawl through existing propositions and design work for 'look and feel' responses. Marketing is, however, preoccupied with the way in which a product or service is focused, how it is received and how people respond to it. Marketing has a tendency to drive the design, so you might say that the market leads and the design follows. This is not always the case though, as there are many instances where design can be the instigating factor.

The impact of marketing on the designer can be prescriptive or restrictive in many ways. Take packaging design, for example; the creation of a physical shape and/or the surface design needs to be supported by a strategy, as the design work will most probably be based on its market position and market placement. The designer will therefore need to work closely with the marketing team within the design company, as well as the marketing department and brand guardians from the client side/company in order to make sure that all the necessary requirements and desires of the client/ company are accurately transposed to the design to procure a successful end result.

When a design or approach has been formalised, it will, with all certainty, be tested for its suitability and accuracy, using focus groups or user groups. These use appropriately

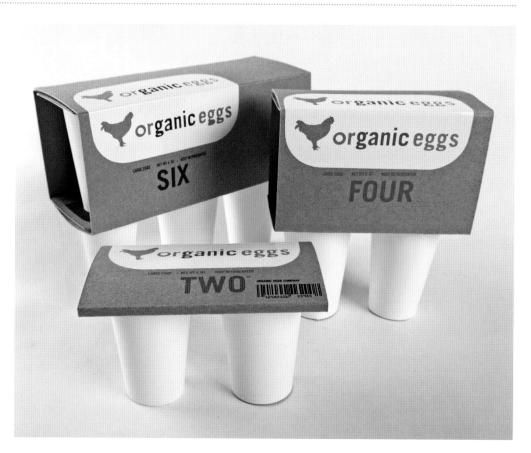

selected consumers or users to provide information and a response to market-focused questions. The sum outcome of this testing can then be translated into success or failure.

Since the advent of the Internet, clients, companies and services can now circumvent certain marketing processes. It is now much easier to have a direct connection to the consumer or user, allowing designers to obtain almost spontaneous feedback through dialogue and evaluation.

With certain services and products, there will always be the question of 'does this need marketing or my creative services to take it to market or not?' Here, it could be a service or product that has an ethical question attached to it. The choice on whether to work on the project or not is for each person to decide, including the consequences as well.

Organic egg packaging ⬆
Lindsey Faye Sherman **(a student at Maryland Institute College of Art, Baltimore, USA)**

This design involved creating a group of packages similar in structure and design to egg packaging, but using limited glue points and designed in units. Each egg carton container was engineered for maximum storage, usability, protection, transportation and storage.

I see graphic design as the organization of information that is semantically correct, syntactically consistent and pragmatically understandable.
Massimo Vignelli

Prototyping

When you have gone through the research process, explored the context and produced a variety of possible conceptual ideas and routes that can be taken forward to a conclusion, the concepts will now need to be reviewed. This will ensure that the ideas are correct and not only answering the brief, but are also a true reflection in design of the brand, company, product or service.

Soliciting feedback is the best way to ascertain progress. This can take the form of 1:1, group or peer-to-peer. Getting other opinions, even if they might appear to be conflicting, will help clarify and substantiate thoughts and approaches with what has been produced so far. Here it is crucial to identify the key strengths of the brand, company, product or service and make sure that they are incorporated and inform the design outcomes.

Minor modifications and alterations may be necessary to the design prototype(s) before things can be progressed; the net result should be a series of variables that fulfill the requirements of the assignment brief. By selecting from these alternatives, further development can take place, to produce a suitable and finished result which will form the basis for testing, presentation or assessment. Only during this activity will it be determined whether the prototype is suitable and accurate as a response.

Design is really a linear process; this is also true with its application. Clear strategies for advancement and production need to be identified. Constantly checking for consistency in the message, for the inclusion of product or service differentiation, and for internationalism/international offering, will increase the chances of the design outcome being correctly and positively perceived.

It is important at this stage to remember that everybody has the right to make mistakes and to learn from them. Trying to please everyone will only dilute a great idea so do not be afraid to put your views forward, even if they might be criticised by others.

Prospectus for University of the Creative Arts ◐
HSAG

The purpose of this prospectus is to give an overview and insight into the current offering of individual courses at the university. The strong design acts as a way of reconfirming the brand proposition and the experience that can be expected when on a course at the university.

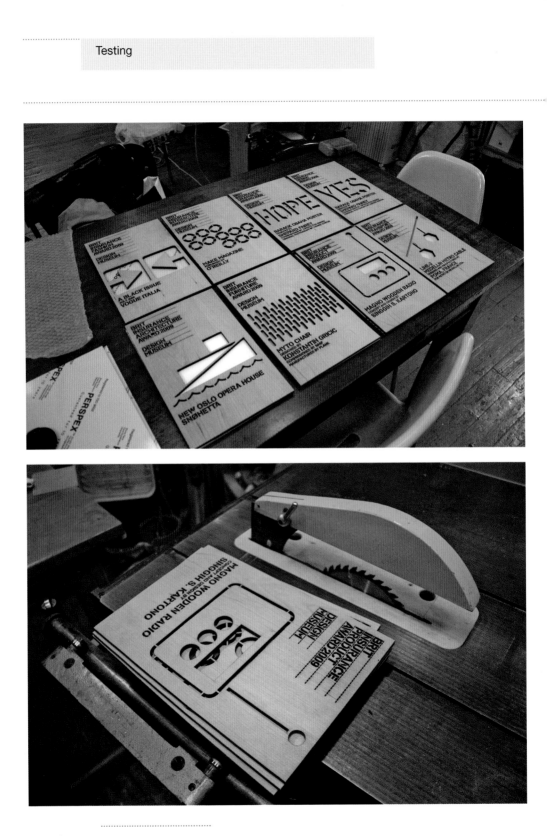

Design Museum Awards ⬆ ⬅ ⬇
Anthony Burrill and *Michael Marriott*

This set of awards, all produced from wood, involve die-cuts which, when cut away, reveal a perspex panel suspended a few millimetres away, creating a soft shadow. In this type of design, you never really know what the product will look like until the final construction.

Presenting ideas

Learning how to present creative work is a key skill for a designer. Whether the presentation is to a client, a tutor at critical appraisal or simply as part of a work review, all the points need to get across. Reasoning and conclusion also need to be made explicit. Getting this wrong could result in the rejection of both ideas and work.

When presenting to a client, it is necessary to make sure that the presentation is not biased in favour of one design route (solution) over the others. The client must have the opportunity to weigh up all possible options. With some clients, it is not uncommon for them to select certain aspects from each individual design solution and request that they be combined to form a single route or outcome. Ideally, a designer prefers a client not to take on their role, but will be willing to negotiate to some degree, or at least discuss it. A 'mix and match' approach to the design piece is not advisable.

As the designer and author of the work, it is important to remain focused and supportive of the work, giving grounded reasoning why creative work is the right solution to the brief and the project. Work should always be mounted on boards, and PowerPoint presentations and self-running QuickTime movies must always be professional. This is true regardless of whether the presentation is taking place in an educational or professional environment.

When discussing and presenting the research or design concepts, think of the target audience or end user. Ask yourself: who? what? where? and when?

Who am I trying to say this to?
What am I trying to say?
Where will it be seen?
When is this for?

In all instances of a final presentation, the work should be immaculately finished. Attention to detail speaks volumes about professionalism and your attitude to the creative process – it's not just about the idea.

Remember, first impressions do count!

Some notes on presenting work

Learning how to present creative work to a client,
commissioner, tutor or in a work review is a core skill for
all designers.

1. **Be prepared**
   Preparation is crucial in every presentation situation. Use
   reasoning and be clear with all explanations. Make sure
   all points are covered and all questions are answered.

2. **Don't present to yourself**
   Engage the audience at all times, pace the presentation
   and allow opportunities for directed questioning. It is
   a common mistake to turn the work towards yourself,
   essentially making it upside-down to the person you
   are presenting to. You should be familiar with the work
   but they are not: make sure the work / sketchbook is
   facing them.

3. **Clarity**
   Speak clearly. If presenting as part of a team, decide
   who will say and do what and when, prior to the start of
   the presentation. Be organised and scripted, use prompt
   cards if necessary.

4. **Visuals**
   Always test all presentation equipment such as
   computers, discs and media with a dry run and before
   starting the presentation. Professionalism counts as well
   as the creative outcomes being shown.

5. **Summing up and closing**
   Try and bring the presentation to a clear conclusion
   with defined outcomes; make notes and capture all
   comments.

Studio interview:

Morag Myerscough

Influential London-based Studio Myerscough produce thoughtful and eclectic solutions to graphic problems. Here, design principal Morag Myerscough gives an insight into her education and her early links to craft and art.

What made you decide to study graphic design/advertising/illustration?

My mum is an embroiderer and my grandmother was a milliner for Hartnells and from a very early age I would sew and do embroidery easily. However, I wanted to do something different.

When I went to do my foundation degree at Central Saint Martin's College of Art and Design in London they put me in classes that were more directed towards design than fine art. I always felt that was a little early to be positioned so definitely, but maybe they were right: if I desperately wanted to be a painter I would have done it. Also, Robin Baggihole was a great tutor and I was introduced to printing, which I loved. I managed to do a litho print with 18 colours!

Who was your most influential tutor/teacher and why?

At the end of my second year, I had a tutor who gave me a glimmer of hope. The year had been too much about designing hankie boxes and I really hadn't found it interesting. However, our new tutor came along, and it all changed after that: we were allowed to think laterally, to go on journeys with our ideas, to analyse and discuss. He opened my mind to what I could do as a designer and he showed me that creativity was not restricted by a discipline – if I wanted to design every aspect of a project I could, not just a cover, or a stamp, or a poster. He showed me that I could shape the project and put my own thoughts forward.

In your point of view, what are the key things to learn on a course or at college?

How to think

How to realise those thoughts

Passion

Enjoy yourself

What makes a student successful at college or as a graduate?

A person who thinks

A person who can begin to realise those thoughts

A person who wants to learn

A person with imagination and enthusiasm

A committed person

A person who likes to laugh

Icon ← ↓

These images are taken from a shoot for a cover of *Icon* magazine and accompany an article on new pioneers in architecture and design. With time and budget constraints, the studio cut 4,000 polystyrene blocks in various lengths and set them in a pixelated, graduated font designed by the studio. The blocks were produced in large numbers so that the photographs could be taken in a space that would provide the image with a sense of scale.

A hybrid can be a combination of anything. So a hybrid idea will be a mixture of two or more previously unrelated concepts. It is a way of producing unexpected patterns of thought or form and can be developed through several generations.

Brief

Select an area of design from list A, which you feel directly relates to your area of interest or practice. Use one of the ideas from List B to create a design for this format.

List A

- Brand/identity
- Diagram/mapping
- Editorial
- Image
- Information
- Mark making
- Packaging
- Type, letterforms and language
- Rich media

List B

- If the *World at One* radio programme was to be combined with garden seed packaging.
- If letterforms were to be crossed with the 40 weeks of human gestation.
- If a prayer was to be turned into a timetable.
- If punctuation was combined with an electrical wiring diagram from a house.
- If documentary photography crossed with algebra.
- If topography was moulded with astrology.

Project objectives

- Experimentation of different ways of making patterns from structural thinking.

Advanced

As part of the final piece, you may wish to consider the hypothesis of how your hybrid could be applied in a real world context, now or in the future.

Recommended reading related to this project

Aldersey-Williams, H. 1990. *Cranbrook Design: The New Discourse*. Rizzoli International Publications

Barthes, R. and Howard, R. 1993. *Camera Lucida: Reflections on Photography*. Vintage

Baudrillard, J. and Glaser, S. 1994. *Simulacra and Simulation, The Body in Theory: Histories of Cultural Materialism*. The University of Michigan Press

Berger, J. 2008. *About Looking*. Bloomsbury Publishing

Hall, S. 2007. *This Means This, This Means That: A User's Guide to Semiotics*. Laurence King

McQuiston, L. 1995. *Graphic Agitation: Social and Political Graphics Since the Sixties*. Phaidon Press Ltd

Rathgeb, M. 2006. *Otl Aicher*. Phaidon Press

Chapter 6 – Conventions

Design, by its very nature, is a creative discipline, but designers will often find themselves working within defined boundaries. These conventions are required to maintain order and balance so a firm understanding of them is vital in order for effective design and communication to take place.

This chapter will introduce some common conventions, such as paper formats, file formats and colour systems.

Several formats are common to graphic design and are important for the production of design work. The UK uses millimetres for general measuring but ISO A/B/C sizes for paper. Points and picas are used in typography (for cold metal setting especially) and offline, print-based media, and bits and pixels are used for online or screen work.

Paper sizes

The ISO paper-size system is now a standard and is used globally when working with paper. These sizes are based on a metric system, and are based on the principles outlined below.

The height of the page is divided by the width, whilst all formats are the square root of two (1.4142). So, for example, A0 (generally the largest paper size commonly used), has an area of one square metre. A1, the next size down, is an A0 sheet cut into two equal pieces. So the height of A1 is the width of A0 and the width of A1 is half the height of A0. All smaller sized sheets of the A system are simply defined by this formulae.

B sizes were introduced to allow for a greater range of paper sizes. The same goes for C sizes, which were introduced for envelopes.

ISO sizes ➡

ISO (international standard) paper series are used in most countries in the world today. They define the A and B series of paper sizes. Each is defined by halving the preceding paper size, cutting parallel to its shorter side.

Aspect ratios ⬇

$1 : \sqrt{2} = 0.707$ – this ratio has a unique property in that when cut or folded in half lengthwise, the halves also have the same aspect ratio. Each ISO paper size is one half of the next size up. This diagram clearly shows the relationship between the page sizes.

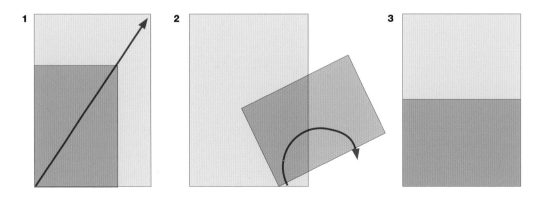

1   2   3

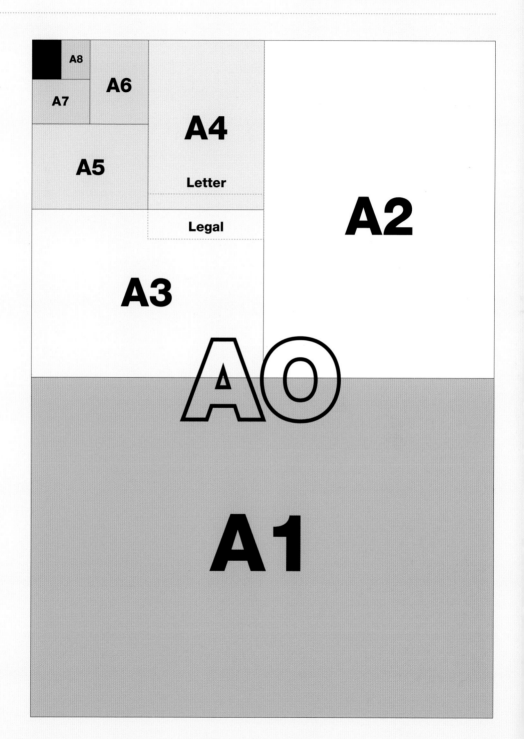

ISO paper sizes (mm)

A series formats:	B series formats:	C series formats:
4A0 1682 × 2378		
2A0 1189 × 1682		
A0 841 × 1189	B0 1000 × 1414	C0 917 × 1297
A1 594 × 841	B1 707 × 1000	C1 648 × 917
A2 420 × 594	B2 500 × 707	C2 458 × 648
A3 297 × 420	B3 353 × 500	C3 324 × 458
A4 210 × 297	B4 250 × 353	C4 229 × 324
A5 148 × 210	B5 176 × 250	C5 162 × 229
A6 105 × 148	B6 125 × 176	C6 114 × 162
A7 74 × 105	B7 88 × 125	C7 81 × 114
A8 52 × 74	B8 62 × 88	C8 57 × 81
A9 37 × 52	B9 44 × 62	C9 40 × 57
A10 26 × 37	B10 31 × 44	C10 28 × 40

US paper sizes

Name	in × in	mm × mm	Ratio	Alias	Similar ISO A size
ANSI A	8½ × 11	216 × 279	1.2941	Letter	A4
ANSI B	17 × 11	432 × 279	1.5455	Ledger	A3
	11 × 17	279 × 432	1.5455	Tabloid	A3
ANSI C	17 × 22	432 × 559	1.2941		A2
ANSI D	22 × 34	559 × 864	1.5455		A1
ANSI E	34 × 44	864 × 1118	1.2941		A0

P4-based series – based on Canadian standards, but also used in international magazine printing

Name	mm × mm	Ratio
PA0	840 × 1120	3:4
PA1	560 × 840	2:3
PA2	420 × 560	3:4
PA3	280 × 420	2:3
PA4	210 × 280	3:4
PA5	140 × 210	2:3
PA6	105 × 140	3:4
PA7	70 × 105	2:3
PA8	52 × 70	≈3:4
PA9	35 × 52	≈2:3
PA10	26 × 35	≈3:4

Paper sizes in general use

Paper size	Application
A0, A1	technical drawings, posters
A1, A2	flip charts
A2, A3	drawings, diagrams, large tables
A4	letters, magazines, forms, catalogues, laser printer and copy-machine output
A5	notepads
A6	postcards
B5, A5, B6, A6	books
C4, C5, C6	envelopes for A4 letters: unfolded (C4), folded once (C5), folded twice (C6)
B4, A3	newspapers, supported by most copy machines in addition to A4
B8, A8	playing cards

Envelope formats

Format	Size (mm)	Content Format
C6	114 × 162	A4 folded twice = A6
DL	110 × 220	A4 folded twice = 1/3 A4
C6/C5	114 × 229	A4 folded twice = 1/3 A4
C5	162 × 229	A4 folded once = A5
C4	229 × 324	A4
C3	324 × 458	A3
B6	125 × 176	C6 envelope
B5	176 × 250	C5 envelope
B4	250 × 353	C4 envelope
E4	280 × 400	B4

The most widely used format for letters is DL.

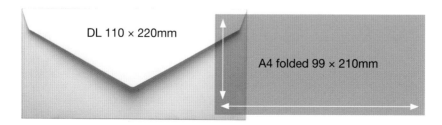

DL 110 × 220mm

A4 folded 99 × 210mm

Points and picas

In Europe in the 1780s, François-Ambroise Didot devised a system for type specification. It was based on a previous system created by Pierre Simon Fournier. Didot altered Fournier's specifications to conform to the French Royal inch or pouce (Fournier's specifications up until that time were not based on a standard measure). Ciceros (the units of Didot's system) are still used in France and other European countries today.

In the UK and USA, points and picas have become standard measurement units. Devised in the USA in 1886, the pica measures 0.1660 inches (just under one sixth of an inch) and a point is 0.0138 inches in length. This is very close to Fournier's original specification, but a little bit less than 1/72 of an inch (1 inch = 25.4 millimetres). There are 12 points in a pica.

Points and picas are used to set measurements of page proportion and type. It is also common for measurements relating to type, for example leading, to be described in points as illustrated below.

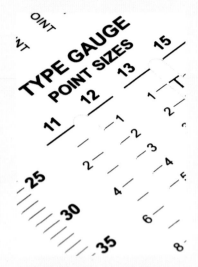

Type gauge ⬆
A type gauge ruler printed on two sides for quick and accurate type specification. Generally, each point size scale has open cut slots to allow for flush-to-the-edge measuring.

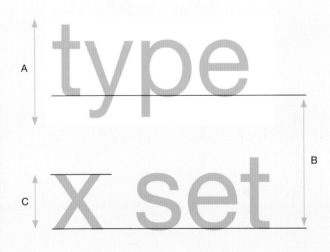

A

B

C

Point size, leading and x-height ⬅
Three common sizes described in points are point size, leading and x-height.

Point size (A) is the measurement from above the ascender to below the descender. This size describes the typeface's 'bounding box' rather than the height of any given character.

Leading (B) is the measurement from the baseline of one line of text to the baseline of the next.

X-height (C) is the measurement from the baseline to the mean line of a typeface. It is generally true that the bigger a typeface's x-height the more legible the font will be, especially at small sizes, for example in newspaper body copy.

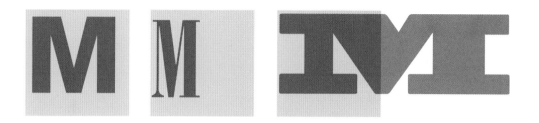

The em and en are also important measurements to consider when dealing with points and picas. Traditionally, in early printing techniques an em was equivalent to the width of an upper-case 'M'. However, in modern typefaces the 'M' is usually somewhat narrower than one em. This unit is not defined in terms of any typeface and is the same for all fonts. So one em in a 12pt typeface would measure 12 points, and one em in a 40pt typeface would measure 40 points. An en is half of this relative measurement.

The en and em are also used as a form of dash, and these have distinct sizes compared to a hyphen, with which they are often confused, as illustrated below.

Em sizes ⬆
Three examples of an 80pt (point), 'M' or 'em'. From left to right: Helvetica, Bodoni and Black Oak (based on a woodblock typeface).

— hyphen

— en dash

— em dash

Design is a linear process – thinking and conceptualising, mark making, reviewing, developing, implementing and evaluating – and as we move through each stage, we need to store and save what we create. Setting up an organised system for filing, storing and retrieving work is vital for all graphic designers. How this is done comes down to personal choice and goes beyond the scope of this book. However, a guide to some common file types is given here to enable more effective organisation sytstems.

Common file types

.bmap Non-compressed image files (bitmaps). These use a grid of small squares known as pixels to represent images.

.doc Written text documents created in Microsoft Word.

.eps (Encapsulated PostScript Files) These files can contain any combination of text, graphics and images.

.gif or .jif (Graphic Interchange Format) These are graphic files that can be easily manipulated by a large number of programs. They are best suited for simpler images.

.indd Adobe® InDesign documents, usually used to create page layouts.

.jpg or jpeg A compressed bitmap image used to display photographs for print or screen.

.pdf (Portable Document Format) An open standard for document exchange. PDF files enable text and images to be easily exchanged.

.png (Portable Network Graphics) These contain a bitmap of indexed colours under a lossless compression. They are generally used for online image/graphics.

.psd Adobe® Photoshop graphic files, which maintain masks, layers, clipping paths, and alpha channels.

.raw Uncompressed, raw image data files used in photography. Exposure and white balance can be edited with software after saving the image to a computer.

.tif Tiff files are platform-independent image files and are therefore highly flexible.

JPEG

image-0012.jpg
800 × 800

text-for-design.doc

mater-file.psd
1,181 × 1,181

Dolly-Italic.bmap

Rasters and vectors

There are two main ways of saving a digital image: as either a raster (or bitmap) or vector.

Rasters and bitmaps are made up of pixels in a grid, each pixel containing colour information. These images have a fixed resolution so it is not possible to re-size them without losing image quality.

Vector images are much more complex and are made up of individual, scalable objects, parts or geometrical primitives: points, lines, curves and shapes. These are all based on mathematical equations and the objects have editable attributes such as colour, fill and outline. Altering a vector image is possible and enlargement will not result in loss of detail.

Rasters and vectore ⬇

In the example below, the difference between vector and raster images can be seen. A vector image can be enlarged to any size without loss of quality or resolution. In contrast, a raster image is a fixed size, and if enlarged too much will result in loss of image resolution.

Vector image   **Raster image**

Halftones

This is the method of producing a range of tones, as found in a photograph or tinted area. A halftone is created by applying a screen to an image, resulting in a conversion of the image into a series of dots. The dark areas will appear in relatively big dots, placed close together, whilst the lighter areas will appear to have small dots surrounded by white space. The final quality of the image is determined by the number of dots used per inch (dpi). For example, the dots (screen) in a newspaper can be easily seen, as the screen used is generally quite coarse (around 60dpi). A full-colour magazine, on the other hand, would use a much finer screen (around 150dpi), and a book such as this one would use a screen of 300dpi.

A bitmap image consists of only one colour, black.

To print photographic tones the image is converted into a series of dots....

... as can be seen here.

Pixels (PPI and DPI)

A pixel is a single point of any raster image. It is also the smallest element of a digital or screen picture. Each individual pixel inhabits its own space on a two-dimensional grid.

Colour depth is represented by bits, as in bits per pixel or bpp; all colours are dependent on the number of bits (1bpp images use one bit for each pixel). A pixel is either active or not. With the addition of each bit, the colour number doubles in size. So a 2bpp colour image will have four colours and a 3bpp image will have six colours. By reducing or increasing the amount of colours, the size of the image file will also increase or decrease. Too few colours will result in what is referred to as dither, a fuzziness or blurring around the edges of an image. Other terms associated with pixels are: dots per inch (dpi) and pixels per inch (ppi).

The size of a pixel is in relation to the screen used. On a high-resolution monitor for instance, the number of pixels increases, although the physical screen size in inches remains the same.

Pixels ⬇

A pixel is a square of information that contains a description of colour and intensity. All raster images are saved in pixels. They are also displayed on screen in pixels, PPI (pixels per inch), but when they print, they print in dots per inch, (DPI), as shown below.

An original image is saved in pixels per inch...

... viewed in pixels...

... and printed in dots per inch.

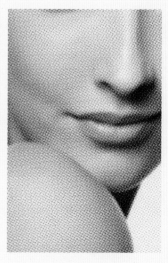

Graphic designers will generally need to be aware of three different colour systems. These are hexadecimal colours (websafe), spot (special) colours (Pantone Matching System or PMS) and process colours (four-colour process or CMYK; CMYK tends to be used for print work and offline use whereas RGB tends to be used for screen and online use).

Hexadecimal colours ⬅
Hexadecimal colours are used for creating colours in HTML (for the web).

White
FFFFFFFF

Dark Olive Green
FF556B2F

Black
FF000000

Hexadecimal colours (websafe)

Hex colours are used when creating design work for the Internet. They contain HTML coding and are defined through a hexadecimal (hex) notation (a combination of red, green and blue colour values). The lowest value that can be used is 0 (hex 00) and the highest value is 255 (hex FF). Hex values are written as three double-digit numbers, starting with a # sign. There are 216 colours commonly considered 'websafe'. Monitors and browsers used to be limited to using a maximum of 256 different colors, but now most computers can display millions of different colours.

Designers have often been encouraged to stick to the 216 websafe colours for websites to avoid colour dither, but due to improvements in computer technology, this is no longer necessarily the case.

Spot or special colours (Pantone Matching System)

Spot colours are used where colour accuracy is key, such as with branding and logos. The standard system used for spot colour work is Pantone, which uses a unique Pantone numbering system to identify colours. It was originally designed for the graphics industry and is now used by a wide range of industries.

The system is divided into C (coated paper), U (uncoated paper), M (matt paper), so a colour would appear on the palette as either Pantone 151 C, Pantone 151 U, or Pantone 151 M, for example. The guide palette allows the designer to select and gauge a colour for print accurately.

Process colours (four-colour process or CMYK)

Process colours or the four-colour set: cyan, magenta, yellow and black (K stands for key – aligning each printing plate to the black plate), are used for the origination of continuous tones (as with colour photographs) through the process of ink on paper.

The three colours cyan, magenta and yellow are overprinted in successive order, before black is added. As the inks are translucent, the result will be in the form of a direct replication of all the full range of colours, as seen in reality.

Pantone colours ⬆
Pantone colours are used when an exact colour match is required.

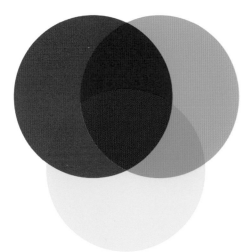

CMYK ⬆
The subtractive primary colours, cyan, magenta and yellow. Where two subtractives overlap, an additive primary (red, green or blue) is created. Where all three overlap, black is created.

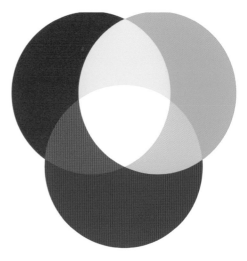

RGB ⬆
The additive primary colours, red, green and blue. Where two additives overlap, a subtractive primary (cyan, magenta or yellow) is produced. Where all three overlap, white is produced.

Print order

Full-colour (four-colour) printing involves a series of necessary steps for the production of a high-quality colour reproduction.

Firstly, the original artwork needs to be separated into its red, green, and blue components. This is usually done with a digital scanner (see pages 92–93). Next, each of these separations is inverted so that a negative of each element is created. The developed negative from each will represent the cyan, magenta and yellow colours respectively.

Cyan, magenta, and yellow are the three main pigments used for full-colour colour reproduction. The combination of these results in a fairly accurate reproduction of the original image. The darkest colours however are usually quite brownish in colour. To achieve a true range of dark tones it is necessary to add a black separation as the fourth colour. This improves the shadow and contrast of the image.

Printing plates ⬇
These images show the order in which an image is usually printed. The image depth and colour builds with the addition of each 'plate'. Notice how the addition of the final black plate adds depth and contrast to the image.

C

CM

CMY

CMYK

Appendix

Here, we suggest some useful sources of information and inspiration for the graphic design student.

This book attempts to give an introduction and overview to the subject of graphic design. Throughout the book we have tried to focus on some of the key processes and aspects of the subject and to show through accompanying visuals and diagrams, from both students and practitioners, a practical insight into the design discipline. The book presents and discusses context and history while also looking at the theoretical and practical considerations associated with the study of graphic design at undergraduate level, or the beginnings of a career in creative practice.

Some of the mechanics involved within the design conceptualisation and development phases are explored – from idea generation techniques, through to the communication of developed ideas. This book should give any graphic design student a solid introduction to the subject, whilst at the same time providing them with the core design language needed in order to respond to any design course content.

We hope you have found the content useful. Here, we give ideas for further research and exploration.

Contributor contacts

Boris Bogdanov, London, UK
www.borislavdizain.tumblr.com

Anthony Burrill, UK
www.anthonyburrill.com

Fred Deakin, Airside, London, UK
www.airside.co.uk

Noel Douglas, London, UK
www.noeldouglas.net

Ben Edwards, UK
www.benjamin-edwards.com

Lindsey Faye Sherman, Baltimore, USA
www.lindseyfaye.com

Will Foley, UK
lone.bee@hotmail.com

Slavimir Stojanovic/Futro studio, Serbia
www.slavimirstojanovic.com

Adam Hayes, London, UK
www.mrahayes.co.uk

Alberto Hernández, London, UK
www.hereigo.co.uk

Dennis Y Ichiyama, Purdue University,
Indiana, USA
www.purdue.edu

IlovarStritar, Ljubljana, Slovenia
www.ilovarstritar.com

Richard Irving, McCann Manchester Limited,
Cheshire, UK
www.mccannmanchester.com

Robert Kennett, Broadstairs, UK

Rodeo Design, Adelaide, Australia
www.hello-rodeo.com

Ben Rix, Brighton, UK
benrix@live.com

Kareena Ross-Cumming, Kent, UK
kareena_icecool@hotmail.com

Dean Samed, Kent, UK
www.conzpiracy.deviantart.com/gallery

Patrick Thomas, Barcelona, Spain
www.patrickthomas.com

Raphaëlle Moreau, Lyon, France
www.raphaelle-moreau.com

Morag Myerscough, Studio Myerscough,
London, UK
www.studiomyerscough.com

Sam Piyasena, Billie Jean, London, UK
www.billiejean.co.uk

Joel Wade, Kent, UK
joel.wade@mac.com

Holly Wales, London. UK
www.eatjapanesefood.co.uk

Charles Wiliams, London, UK
www.unclecharles.co.uk

Sara Yates, Leeds, UK
www.sarayates.blogspot.com

Lawrence Zeegen, School of
Communication Design,
Kingston University, UK
www.kingston.ac.uk
www.zeegen.com

Zek Crew, Ljubljana, Slovenia
www.zek.si

Bibliography

Aldersey-Williams, H. 1990. *Cranbrook Design: The New Discourse.* Rizzoli International Publications.

Badger, G. 2007. *The Genius of Photography.* Quadrille Publishing.

Baines, P. 2005. *Penguin by Design: A Cover Story 1935–2005.* Allen Lane.

Barthes, R. 2009. *Mythologies.* Vintage Classics.

Barthes, R. and Howard, R. 1993. *Camera Lucida: Reflections on Photography.* Vintage.

Baudrillard, J. and Glaser, S. 1994. *Simulacra and Simulation, The Body in Theory: Histories of Cultural Materialism.* The University of Michigan Press.

Bayley, S. 2008. *Life's a Pitch.* Roger Mavity, Corgi Books.

Bayley, S. and Mavity, R. 2008. *Life's a Pitch.* Corgi Books.

Berger, J. 2008. *About Looking.* Bloomsbury Publishing.

Berger, J. 2008. *Ways of Seeing.* Penguin Classics.

Brereton, R. 2009. *Sketchbooks: The Hidden Art of Designers, Illustrators & Creatives.* Laurence King.

Bringhurst, R. 2004. The *Elements of Typographic Style.* Hartley & Marks Publishers.

Buxton, B. 2007. *Sketching User Experiences: Getting the Design Right and the Right Design.* Morgan Kaufmann.

Carson, D. and L. Blackwell, L. 1995. *The End of Print: The Graphic Design of David Carson.* Chronicle Books.

Chandler, D. 2002. *Semiotics: The Basics.* Routledge.

Crowley, D. 2008. *Cold War Modern: Design 1945–1970.* Victoria & Albert Museum.

Davis, J. 2002. *Flash to the Core: An Interactive Sketchbook.* New Riders.

De Bono, E. 1967. *The Use of Lateral Thinking.* Jonathan Cape.

Derrida, J. 2001. *Writing and Difference.* Routledge Classics, Routledge.

Fawcett-Tang, R. 2008. *Mapping Graphic Navigational Systems.* Rotovision.

Foucault, M. 1994. *The Order of Things.* Random House.

Geisler, H. and Pabst, J. 2007. *Karl Gerstner: Designing Programmes.* Lars Muller Publishers.

Glaser, M. 2006. *The Design of Dissent: Socially and Politically Driven Graphics.* Rockport Publishers Inc.

Godfrey, J.and Heller, S. 2009. *BiblioGraphic: 100 Classic Graphic Design Books.* Laurence King.

Hall, S. 2007. *This Means This, This Means That: A User's Guide to Semiotics.* Laurence King.

Harmon, K. 2003. *You are Here: Personal Geographies and Other Maps of the Imagination.* Princeton Architectural Press.

Heller, S. 2008. *Iron Fists: Branding the 20th-Century Totalitarian State.* Phaidon Press Inc.

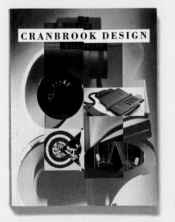

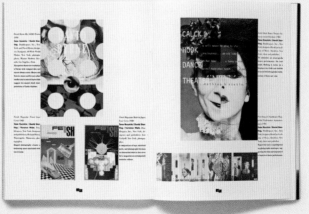

Herbert, S. 2004. *Pioneers of Modern Typography.* Lund Humphries Publishers Ltd.

Hofmann, A. 2009. *Graphic Design Manual: Aufbau - Synthese - Anwendung.* Niggli Verlag.

Hollis, R. 2001. *Concise History of Graphic Design.* Thames & Hudson.

Imber, J. 2000. *Dictionary of Marketing Terms (Barron's Business Guides).* Barron's Educational Series.

Itten, J. 1975. *Design and Form: Basic Course at the Bauhaus.* John Wiley & Sons.

Itten, J. 1970. *The Elements of Color: A Treatise on the Color System of Johannes Itten, Based on His Book "The Art of Color".* John Wiley & Sons.

Kane, J. 2002. *A Type Primer.* Laurence King.

Klein, N. 2001. *No Logo: No Space. No Choice. No Jobs.* Flamingo.

Laurel, B. 2003. *Design Research Methods and Perspectives.* MIT Press.

Lupton, E. 1999. *Design Writing Research.* Phaidon Press.

Lupton, E. and Abbott Miller J. 1993. *The ABCs of the Bauhaus: The Bauhaus and Design Theory.* Thames & Hudson.

McLuhan, M. and Fiore, Q. 2008. *The Medium is the Massage: An Inventory of Effects.* Penguin Classics.

McQuiston, L. 1995. *Graphic Agitation: Social and Political Graphics Since the Sixties.* Phaidon Press Ltd.

Meggs, P. and Purvis, A. 2006. *A History of Graphic Design.* John Wiley & Sons.

Moggridge, B. 2006. *Designing Interactions.* MIT Press.

Muller-Brockmann, J. 2009. *Grid Systems in Graphic Design: A Handbook for Graphic Artists, Typographers, and Exhibition Designers.* Niggli Verlag.

Muller-Brockmann, J. 2000. *Pioneer of Swiss Graphic Design.* Lars Muller Publishers.

Napper T. Q. and Monheim, F. 2002. *LOMO: Don't Think *Just Shoot: Leningradskoye Optiko Mechanichesckoye Obyedinenie: (Major American ... PhD Qualifying Questions and Solutions).* Booth-Clibborn Editions.

Poyner, R. and Spencer, H. 2004. *Pioneers of Modern Typography.* Lund Humphries Publishers.

Rathgeb, M. 2006. *Otl Aicher.* Phaidon Press.

Rees, D. and Blechman, N. 2008. *How to be an Illustrator.* Laurence King.

Tschichold, J. 2006. *The New Typography, Weimar and Now: German Cultural Criticism.* University of California Press.

Tufte, E. R. 1990. *Envisioning Information.* Graphics Press.

VanderLans , R. and Licko, Z. and Gray, M. E. and Keedy, J. 1994. *Emigre (The Book): Graphic Design into the Digital Realm.* John Wiley & Sons Inc.

Weingart, W. 1999. *Weingart: Typography - My Way to Typography: Retrospective in Ten Chapters.* Lars Muller Publishers.

Index

Index compiled by
Indexing Specialists (UK) Ltd.
www.indexing.co.uk

I would like to thank the following people for their generosity of time and support throughout the writing and creation of this book: Hiroko and India Aono-Billson, family and friends. Paul Crawley, Fred Deakin, Richard Doust, Dennis Y Ichiyama, Ronald Lagendijk, Morag Myerscough, Neil Sloman, Faydherbe/de Vringer, Lawrence Zeegen. Leafy Robinson, Caroline Walmsley and Brian Morris at AVA Publishing for their engagement, interest and support.

For allowing the reproduction of their work and for their contribution:

Boris Bogdanov, Anthony Burrill, Fred Deakin & Airside, Noel Douglas, Ben Edwards, Lindsey Faye Sherman, Will Foley, Slavimir Stojanovic/Futro studio, Adam Hayes, HSAG, London, UK, Alberto Hernández, Dennis Y Ichiyama, ilovarstritar, Richard Irving, Robert Kennett, Rodeo Design, Ben Rix, Kareena Ross-Cumming, Dean Samed, Patrick Thomas, Propaganda, Raphaëlle Moreau, Morag Myerscough, Sam Piyasena (Billy Jean), Small, London, UK, Faydherbe/de Vringer, Joel Wade, Holly Wales, Charles Wiliams, Sara Yates, Lawrence Zeegen, Zek Crew.

Always just a beginning.

The publisher would like to thank Jeffrey Tribe and Barrie Tullett for their comments on the manuscript.

Image credits

Cover image by Nigel Aono-Billson
p14 Postcard for the Bauhaus Exhibition, July–September 1923 (colour litho) by Wassily Kandinsky (1866–1944). Private collection / courtesy of Swann Auction Galleries / The Bridgeman Art Library / © ADAGP, Paris and DACS, London 2010
p27 Cover design for the poem 'About This' by Vladimir Mayakovsky (litho) by Alexander Rodchenko (1891–1956). Private collection / The Bridgeman Art Library / © Rodchenko & Stepanova Archive, DACS 2010
p63 © Tate, London 2010. Copyright: Ed Ruscha
p101 Poster advertising B.O.A.C. Airways, printed by McCoquodale & Company, London, c.1950 (colour litho) by Beverley Pick (fl.1950s). Private collection / DaTo Images / The Bridgeman Art Library

Publisher's note

The subject of ethics is not new, yet its consideration within the applied visual arts is perhaps not as prevalent as it might be. Our aim here is to help a new generation of students, educators and practitioners find a methodology for structuring their thoughts and reflections in this vital area.

AVA Publishing hopes that these **Working with ethics** pages provide a platform for consideration and a flexible method for incorporating ethical concerns in the work of educators, students and professionals. Our approach consists of four parts:

The **introduction** is intended to be an accessible snapshot of the ethical landscape, both in terms of historical development and current dominant themes.

The **framework** positions ethical consideration into four areas and poses questions about the practical implications that might occur. Marking your response to each of these questions on the scale shown will allow your reactions to be further explored by comparison.

The **case study** sets out a real project and then poses some ethical questions for further consideration. This is a focus point for a debate rather than a critical analysis so there are no predetermined right or wrong answers.

A selection of **further reading** for you to consider areas of particular interest in more detail.

Ethical: aware-
ness/
reflect-
ion/
debate

Working with ethics

Introduction

Ethics is a complex subject that interlaces the idea of responsibilities to society with a wide range of considerations relevant to the character and happiness of the individual. It concerns virtues of compassion, loyalty and strength, but also of confidence, imagination, humour and optimism. As introduced in ancient Greek philosophy, the fundamental ethical question is: *what should I do?* How we might pursue a 'good' life not only raises moral concerns about the effects of our actions on others, but also personal concerns about our own integrity.

In modern times the most important and controversial questions in ethics have been the moral ones. With growing populations and improvements in mobility and communications, it is not surprising that considerations about how to structure our lives together on the planet should come to the forefront. For visual artists and communicators, it should be no surprise that these considerations will enter into the creative process.

Some ethical considerations are already enshrined in government laws and regulations or in professional codes of conduct. For example, plagiarism and breaches of confidentiality can be punishable offences. Legislation in various nations makes it unlawful to exclude people with disabilities from accessing information or spaces. The trade of ivory as a material has been banned in many countries. In these cases, a clear line has been drawn under what is unacceptable.

But most ethical matters remain open to debate, among experts and lay-people alike, and in the end we have to make our own choices on the basis of our own guiding principles or values. Is it more ethical to work for a charity than for a commercial company? Is it unethical to create something that others find ugly or offensive?

Specific questions such as these may lead to other questions that are more abstract. For example, is it only effects on humans (and what they care about) that are important, or might effects on the natural world require attention too?

Is promoting ethical consequences justified even when it requires ethical sacrifices along the way? Must there be a single unifying theory of ethics (such as the Utilitarian thesis that the right course of action is always the one that leads to the greatest happiness of the greatest number), or might there always be many different ethical values that pull a person in various directions?

As we enter into ethical debate and engage with these dilemmas on a personal and professional level, we may change our views or change our view of others. The real test though is whether, as we reflect on these matters, we change the way we act as well as the way we think. Socrates, the 'father' of philosophy, proposed that people will naturally do 'good' if they know what is right. But this point might only lead us to yet another question: *how do we know what is right?*

You
What are your ethical beliefs?

Central to everything you do will be your attitude to people and issues around you. For some people, their ethics are an active part of the decisions they make every day as a consumer, a voter or a working professional. Others may think about ethics very little and yet this does not automatically make them unethical. Personal beliefs, lifestyle, politics, nationality, religion, gender, class or education can all influence your ethical viewpoint.

Using the scale, where would you place yourself? What do you take into account to make your decision? Compare results with your friends or colleagues.

Your client
What are your terms?

Working relationships are central to whether ethics can be embedded into a project, and your conduct on a day-to-day basis is a demonstration of your professional ethics. The decision with the biggest impact is whom you choose to work with in the first place. Cigarette companies or arms traders are often-cited examples when talking about where a line might be drawn, but rarely are real situations so extreme. At what point might you turn down a project on ethical grounds and how much does the reality of having to earn a living affect your ability to choose?

Using the scale, where would you place a project? How does this compare to your personal ethical level?

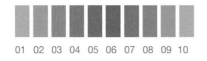

01 02 03 04 05 06 07 08 09 10

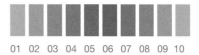

01 02 03 04 05 06 07 08 09 10

Your specifications
What are the impacts of your materials?

In relatively recent times, we are learning that many natural materials are in short supply. At the same time, we are increasingly aware that some man-made materials can have harmful, long-term effects on people or the planet. How much do you know about the materials that you use? Do you know where they come from, how far they travel and under what conditions they are obtained? When your creation is no longer needed, will it be easy and safe to recycle? Will it disappear without a trace? Are these considerations your responsibility or are they out of your hands?

Using the scale, mark how ethical your material choices are.

Your creation
What is the purpose of your work?

Between you, your colleagues and an agreed brief, what will your creation achieve? What purpose will it have in society and will it make a positive contribution? Should your work result in more than commercial success or industry awards? Might your creation help save lives, educate, protect or inspire? Form and function are two established aspects of judging a creation, but there is little consensus on the obligations of visual artists and communicators toward society, or the role they might have in solving social or environmental problems. If you want recognition for being the creator, how responsible are you for what you create and where might that responsibility end?

Using the scale, mark how ethical the purpose of your work is.

01 02 03 04 05 06 07 08 09 10   01 02 03 04 05 06 07 08 09 10

Working with ethics

One aspect of graphic design that raises an ethical dilemma is that of its relationship with the creation of printed materials and the environmental impacts of print production. For example, in the UK, it is estimated that around 5.4 billion items of addressed direct mail are sent out every year and these, along with other promotional inserts, amount to over half a million tonnes of paper annually (almost 5 per cent of the UK consumption of paper and board). Response rates to mail campaigns are known to be between 1–3 per cent, making junk mail arguably one of the least environmentally friendly forms of print communication. As well as the use of paper or board, the design decisions to use scratch-off panels, heavily coated gloss finishes, full-colour ink-intensive graphics or glues for seals or fixings make paper more difficult to recycle once it has been discarded. How much responsibility should a graphic designer have in this situation if a client has already chosen to embark on a direct mail campaign and has a format in mind? Even if designers wish to minimise the environmental impacts of print materials, what might they most usefully do?

In 1951, Leo Burnett (the famous advertising executive known for creating the Jolly Green Giant and the Marlboro Man) was hired to create a campaign for Kellogg's new cereal, Sugar Frosted Flakes (now Frosties in the UK and Frosted Flakes in the US). Tony the Tiger, designed by children's book illustrator Martin Provensen, was one of four characters selected to sell the cereal. Newt the Gnu and Elmo the Elephant never made it to the shelves and after Tony proved more popular than Katy the Kangaroo, she was dropped from packs after the first year.

Whilst the orange-and-black tiger stripes and the red kerchief have remained, Provensen's original design for Tony has changed significantly since he first appeared in 1952. Tony started out with an American football-shaped head, which later became more rounded, and his eye colour changed from green to gold. Today, his head is more angular and he sits on a predominantly blue background. Tony was initially presented as a character that walked on all fours and was no bigger than a cereal box. By the 1970s, Tony's physique had developed into a slim and muscular six-foot-tall standing figure.

Between 1952 and 1995 Kellogg's are said to have spent more than USD$1 billion promoting Frosted Flakes with Tony's image, while generating USD$5.3 billion in gross US sales. But surveys by consumer rights groups such as Which? find that over 75 per cent of people believe that using characters on packaging makes it hard for parents to say no to their children. In these surveys, Kellogg's come under specific scrutiny for Frosties, which are said to contain one third sugar and more salt than the Food Standards Agency recommends. In response, Kellogg's have said: 'We are committed to responsibly marketing our brands and communicating their intrinsic qualities so that our customers can make informed choices.'

Food campaigners claim that the use of cartoon characters is a particularly manipulative part of the problem and governments should stop them being used on less healthy children's foods. But in 2008, spokespeople for the Food and Drink Federation in the UK, said: 'We are baffled as to why Which? wants to take all the fun out of food by banning popular brand characters, many of whom have been adding colour to supermarket shelves for more than 80 years.'

Is it more ethical to create promotional graphics for 'healthy' rather than 'unhealthy' food products?

Is it unethical to design cartoon characters to appeal to children for commercial purposes?

Would you have worked on this project, either now or in the 1950s?

I studied graphic design in Germany, and my professor emphasised the responsibility that designers and illustrators have towards the people they create things for.

Eric Carle (illustrator)

Working with ethics

AIGA
Design Business and Ethics
2007, AIGA

Eaton, Marcia Muelder
Aesthetics and the Good Life
1989, Associated University Press

Ellison, David
Ethics and Aesthetics in European Modernist Literature:
From the Sublime to the Uncanny
2001, Cambridge University Press

Fenner, David E W (Ed)
Ethics and the Arts:
An Anthology
1995, Garland Reference Library of Social Science

Gini, Al and Marcoux, Alexei M
Case Studies in Business Ethics
2005, Prentice Hall

McDonough, William and Braungart, Michael
Cradle to Cradle:
Remaking the Way We Make Things
2002, North Point Press

Papanek, Victor
Design for the Real World:
Making to Measure
1972, Thames & Hudson

United Nations Global Compact
The Ten Principles
www.unglobalcompact.org/AboutTheGC/TheTenPrinciples/index.html